AF686502

ECONOMIC ISSUES, PROBLEMS AND PERSPECTIVES

TAX DISTRIBUTION AND REVENUE ANALYSES FOR INDIVIDUAL INCOME TAX

ECONOMIC ISSUES, PROBLEMS AND PERSPECTIVES

Additional books in this series can be found on Nova's website under the Series tab.

Additional E-books in this series can be found on Nova's website under the E-books tab.

ECONOMIC ISSUES, PROBLEMS AND PERSPECTIVES

TAX DISTRIBUTION AND REVENUE ANALYSES FOR INDIVIDUAL INCOME TAX

ANTHONY N. TREVISO
EDITOR

Nova Science Publishers, Inc.
New York

Copyright © 2011 by Nova Science Publishers, Inc.

All rights reserved. No part of this book may be reproduced, stored in a retrieval system or transmitted in any form or by any means: electronic, electrostatic, magnetic, tape, mechanical photocopying, recording or otherwise without the written permission of the Publisher.

For permission to use material from this book please contact us:
Telephone 631-231-7269; Fax 631-231-8175
Web Site: http://www.novapublishers.com

NOTICE TO THE READER

The Publisher has taken reasonable care in the preparation of this book, but makes no expressed or implied warranty of any kind and assumes no responsibility for any errors or omissions. No liability is assumed for incidental or consequential damages in connection with or arising out of information contained in this book. The Publisher shall not be liable for any special, consequential, or exemplary damages resulting, in whole or in part, from the readers' use of, or reliance upon, this material. Any parts of this book based on government reports are so indicated and copyright is claimed for those parts to the extent applicable to compilations of such works.

Independent verification should be sought for any data, advice or recommendations contained in this book. In addition, no responsibility is assumed by the publisher for any injury and/or damage to persons or property arising from any methods, products, instructions, ideas or otherwise contained in this publication.

This publication is designed to provide accurate and authoritative information with regard to the subject matter covered herein. It is sold with the clear understanding that the Publisher is not engaged in rendering legal or any other professional services. If legal or any other expert assistance is required, the services of a competent person should be sought. FROM A DECLARATION OF PARTICIPANTS JOINTLY ADOPTED BY A COMMITTEE OF THE AMERICAN BAR ASSOCIATION AND A COMMITTEE OF PUBLISHERS.

Additional color graphics may be available in the e-book version of this book.

Library of Congress Cataloging-in-Publication Data

Tax distribution and revenue analyses for individual income taxes / editors, Anthony N. Treviso.
p. cm.
Includes index.
ISBN 978-1-61324-421-0 (hardcover)
1. Income tax--United States. 2. Revenue--United States. 3. Tax incidence--United States. I. Treviso, Anthony N.
HJ4652.T354 2011
336.240973--dc22
2011013407

Published by Nova Science Publishers, Inc. † New York

CONTENTS

PREFACE

Distributional effects are often central policy issues in debates over tax legislation. Although economic analysis can be used to estimate the distribution of the tax system, or a tax change, it cannot be used to provide a normative or prescriptive analysis. Descriptive analyses indicate the expected effects of policies, but normative analyses indicate the optimal policy. This book discusses different philosophies about how the tax burden should be distributed, and what those philosophies imply for the shape of the tax system. It addresses the question of the justifications for a progressive tax system, as well as the measures that can be used to characterize the distributional effects of tax changes.

Chapter 1 - Distributional issues often lie at the center of tax policy debates. Distributional analysis may address several issues: How should the tax burden be distributed or, are progressive (increasing as a share of income as income rises) taxes justified? What is the estimated distribution of the current system? How does a particular proposal change that distribution?

Unlike many analyses that study optimal behavior related to allocative issues and economic efficiency, economic analysis cannot be used to answer the questions of how the tax burden should be distributed. Such an answer would depend on social preferences. Economic analysis can, however, identify trade-offs and frame the issue analytically. For example, a number of plausible answers to this question could justify progressive tax structures.

Chapter 2 - While the extent of income inequality is debated periodically, one rarely discussed aspect of inequality is its impact on the tax system. Given the nature of the U.S. federal tax system, changes in the distribution of income can have significant implications for who pays the taxes, how much they pay, and federal tax revenues.

One common measure to characterize inequality or the dispersion of income is the Gini coefficient, which varies from 0 to 1. A Gini coefficient of 0 indicates that income is evenly distributed among the population (that is, everyone has the same income) while a value of 1 indicates perfect income inequality (that is, one individual has all the income). Between 1980 and 2004, the Gini coefficient for household income increased from 0.403 to 0.466—a 15.6% increase. The Gini coefficient for earnings increased by 22.4% from 0.331 in 1980 to 0.405 by 2004. Inequality has, therefore, increased over the past 25 years.

Chapter 3 - Federal individual income tax revenues have risen and fallen by significant amounts since 1994. Revenues increased by $461 billion (85 percent) between fiscal years 1994 and 2000, fell by $211 billion (21 percent) between 2000 and 2003, and then increased by $370 billion (47 percent) between 2003 and 2007. Those changes in individual income tax revenues are partially responsible for a similar pattern in the overall budget balance.

Chapter 4 - Each January in *The Budget and Economic Outlook*, the Congressional Budget Office (CBO) publishes its projections of federal revenues spanning 11 years: the current fiscal year (that is, the fiscal year already under way at that point), the "budget year" (that is, the first full year after the year in which the projections are produced), and the nine fiscal years that follow. Those projections incorporate the assumption that the laws affecting revenues remain unchanged.[1] Since 1997, receipts of individual income taxes have differed from CBO's January projections for the current year by an average of about 6 percent—or by an average of 0.4 percent of gross domestic product (GDP). On average, receipts of individual income taxes for the budget year have differed from the projections made in January of the previous year by about 11 percent (1.0 percent of GDP). All of those differences have been calculated so that they exclude the effects of legislation enacted after the projections were prepared. They have also been calculated without regard to whether the discrepancies were positive or negative—that is, whether CBO overestimated or underestimated actual receipts— and are known as mean absolute errors.[2]

In: Tax Distribution and Revenue Analyses... ISBN: 978-1-61324-421-0
Editor: Anthony N. Treviso © 2011 Nova Science Publishers, Inc.

Chapter 1

DISTRIBUTION OF THE TAX BURDEN ACROSS INDIVIDUALS: AN OVERVIEW*

Jane G. Gravelle

SUMMARY

Distributional issues often lie at the center of tax policy debates. Distributional analysis may address several issues: How should the tax burden be distributed or, are progressive (increasing as a share of income as income rises) taxes justified? What is the estimated distribution of the current system? How does a particular proposal change that distribution?

Unlike many analyses that study optimal behavior related to allocative issues and economic efficiency, economic analysis cannot be used to answer the questions of how the tax burden should be distributed. Such an answer would depend on social preferences. Economic analysis can, however, identify trade-offs and frame the issue analytically. For example, a number of plausible answers to this question could justify progressive tax structures.

Methodological issues, such as the income classifier, the unit of analysis, and assumptions regarding incidence all affect the estimates of the distribution of the current tax burden. Yet all show a similar qualitative result: the federal tax system is progressive throughout its range, although it tends to get much flatter at the top. This pattern is

---

* This is an edited, reformatted and augmented version of a Congressional Research Services publication, CRS Report for Congress RL32693, from www.crs.gov, dated December 17, 2010.

primarily due to the individual income tax, which is quite progressive, and actually provides subsidies at lower-income levels. The other major tax is the payroll tax, which is a larger burden than the individual income tax for more than 80% of the population. This tax is first progressive and then regressive (effective tax rates fall with income). The corporate income and the estate taxes, while much smaller, are also progressive, whereas excise taxes are regressive. This overall progressive pattern has been in place historically, and is expected to continue in the future, although effective tax rates are currently low compared with other periods.

Unlike the federal tax system, state and local taxes tend to be regressive. Thus, a progressive federal tax system would be necessary to prevent overall U.S. taxes from being regressive. The combined taxes appear slightly progressive. Looking at taxes from a lifetime perspective would move the system more toward a proportional tax because average lifetime incomes reduces the variability of income. Studies have suggested that overall lifetime taxes are roughly proportional to income.

Many different measures have been used to characterize the effects of a particular tax change on the distribution of income. A very different impression of tax changes may be obtained depending on the measure used. One popular measure, the percentage change in tax, can be misleading, because as taxes become very small even a negligible absolute change in taxes leads to a very large percentage change. For measuring the relative distribution of income, percentage change in disposable income provides a better measure of how resources are distributed. By this measure, the recent tax cuts made incomes less equal.

INTRODUCTION

Distributional effects are often central policy issues in debates over tax legislation. Although economic analysis can be used to estimate the distribution of the tax system, or a tax change (a positive or descriptive analysis), it cannot be used to provide a normative or prescriptive analysis. Descriptive analyses indicate the expected effects of policies, but normative analyses indicate the optimal policy. Most normative analysis in economics is focused on efficiency. Even in the case of distribution issues, however, economic analysis can be used to facilitate the understanding of desirable distributions, measure them correctly, and determine the implications of different assumptions about social welfare for the optimal distribution of the tax burden.

The first section of this report, which is normative in nature, therefore discusses different philosophies about how the tax burden should be distributed, and what those philosophies imply for the shape of the tax system. In particular, it addresses the question of the justifications for a progressive tax system (one where the share of income collected as a tax rises as income rises). This section is presented for the interested reader, but is not a necessary preliminary to examining the analysis in the second section, which presents estimates of the distribution of the federal and total U.S. tax burden. The third section of the report discusses the measures that can be used to characterize the distributional effects of tax changes.

IS A PROGRESSIVE FEDERAL TAX STRUCTURE JUSTIFIED?

There are two separate, albeit related, questions about tax burden distribution. One of them is how to pay for the goods that the government provides (such as national defense, or highways). The second issue is whether the tax system should be used for direct income redistribution; in that case the optimal tax burden depends on the degree to which redistribution is deemed desirable.

How Should Taxes be Levied to Pay for Government Spending?

Even if an economy had no redistribution, it would be necessary to provide "public goods" (such as defense or roads) and to determine how taxes should be collected to pay for these goods. A public good, in its purest form, is one that each person can enjoy without detracting from anyone else's consumption and where there is no way to exclude a person from enjoying it. As a result of the last effect, in most cases, such goods would not be provided by the private market or would not be provided efficiently.

Many goods are not pure public goods, but have aspects of public goods in that person A benefits from person B's expenditure—such quasi-public goods (or goods with positive external effects) would be provided in the private economy but not in sufficient amounts. To supply these and pure public goods, it is necessary to raise revenues through taxes and distribute the resultant taxes' burden somehow among the society's members.

The distribution of the tax burden with respect to taxpayers' incomes may be characterized as progressive, proportional, or regressive. The behavior of the effective tax rate—the share of income paid in taxes—determines this classification. If the share rises with income, the distribution is called progressive; if it stays constant, it is proportional; and if the share falls, the distribution is called regressive.

Federal taxes, taken one by one, fall into all of the three categories. For the working population, the payroll tax is first proportional, then regressive, because its rate falls once the ceiling of taxable wages is reached. For the population as a whole, the payroll tax rate rises initially, and would therefore be first progressive, then essentially proportional, and for higher-income ranges, regressive. Excise and sales taxes are generally regressive, especially those imposed on products primarily consumed by lower-income individuals, such as cigarettes. The income tax is progressive, and even provides subsidies (negative taxes) for lower-income working individuals, often through the earned income credit. The corporate income tax is imposed on corporate profits as a proportional tax, but its burden on individuals depends on behavioral responses, as discussed subsequently in the "Incidence assumptions" subsection of this report.

Most people would judge that a tax-collection system is fair if it satisfies two limited criteria: horizontal and vertical equity. The criteria state respectively that it is desirable (1) for taxpayers with the same "capacity to pay" to face the same tax liability in dollar terms and (2) for liability to increase with ability to pay. The application of both depends critically on definitions of the same "capacity to pay," which is difficult to determine for the families of different size and other characteristics.

Even under a regressive tax system, a higher-income taxpayer may pay higher taxes in dollar terms than a lower-income taxpayer. What decreases is the share of the tax paid to the income. Therefore a regressive system could still satisfy the principles of vertical and horizontal equity.

Two Alternative Principles of Burden Distribution

Traditionally, there are two theoretical notions of how tax payments should be assigned. One is the benefit principle and another is the "ability-to-pay" principle.

Benefit Principle

The benefit principle simply states that taxpayers who benefit from government services should bear the burden of the tax used to finance the services. The benefit principle seemingly has its roots in market-inspired solutions to paying for public goods. It is commonly associated with such taxes as the gasoline tax, used to finance highways. Although such taxes are not voluntary, as free-market purchases are, they are directly related to the value individuals receive from public goods.

The benefit principle has a much broader reach, if one allows individuals to pay variable prices reflecting their willingness to pay, rather than each individual paying the same amount.[1] Higher-income individuals have a greater willingness to pay for social goods because they have more income. They also might find some goods, such as defense and police protection, more valuable because they have more property to protect.

Under this principle, the distribution may be regressive, proportional, or progressive, depending on whether the taxpayers' income elasticity is greater than, equal to, or less than the price elasticity.[2] Unfortunately, it is difficult to estimate these elasticities, particularly for national level expenditures where there is no cross-sectional variation. Some studies of municipal spending or spending on local education generally indicate that income elasticity exceeds the price elasticity, providing some support for progressive taxes using the benefit principle.[3] There is also some international evidence that tax shares rise as income rises: according to the World Bank[4], high-income countries have taxes as a share of output that are over twice as high as low-income countries, and expenditure shares that are almost twice as large.

Ability to Pay

The "ability-to-pay" principle suggests that people with higher incomes should pay more than those with lower incomes. Yet the standard does not answer the question of how much more. Its policy implications are based on a diminishing marginal benefit of a dollar assumption—the widely accepted belief that the value of an additional dollar of income falls, as income rises (i.e., a rich man values an additional dollar less than a poor).

Notions of ability to pay have generally appealed to some measure of equal sacrifice. Potential measures of "equal sacrifice" include equal absolute sacrifice (each person's welfare declines by the same amount), equal proportional sacrifice (each person's welfare declines by the same proportion), and equal marginal sacrifice (each person's "displeasure" from taking away an additional dollar is the same).

Equal absolute sacrifice would suggest proportional taxation if the marginal benefits of a dollar of income fell proportionally with income. That is, following this principle, if person A with five times as much income as person B values a dollar approximately a fifth as much as B, then for every dollar one collects from B, one collects $5 from A. In this example, the principle implied a proportional tax system. If the marginal benefit of a dollar diminishes, but at a fairly slow rate, a regressive tax system could also be consistent with the principle, whereas if it diminishes at a faster rate, a progressive tax would be appropriate.

An alternative measure of sacrifice is equal proportional sacrifice. This method is much more likely to justify a progressive tax system, but it too depends on how fast the value of an additional dollar declines with income. There are many reasonable functional forms that do not support progressivity.[5]

The equal marginal sacrifice principle suggests steeply progressive taxes that will collect the least valued dollars in the economy. The result also uses the assumption that the value of a dollar falls as income rises. Under this principle, in contrast with the previous two cases, the progressivity does not depend on the rate with which the value declines.

Thus, without further information on the nature of welfare and the exact standard to be used, the ability to pay criterion does not necessarily justify regressive, proportional, or progressive taxes. The equal marginal sacrifice principle suggests an extreme degree of progression.

Distribution as a Public Good

Before discussing general principles of a "just" income distribution, direct redistribution itself as a public good is discussed.

There is normally a natural conflict between equity and efficiency objectives when the equity criterion suggests redistribution or progressive tax rates. That conflict occurs because taxes distort behavior and reduce economic efficiency. It means that the "size of the pie" becomes smaller. There are, however, circumstances in which redistribution can enhance rather than reduce efficiency—when redistribution itself is a public good. Recall that a pure public good can be characterized as a good where one person can benefit from the good without detracting from another's benefit.

Redistribution can, in fact, be characterized as a public good.[6] Suppose that higher and middle income individuals care about the poor and their welfare—that is, they benefit from knowing that the poor have more income.

In this case, redistribution is a public good because A's contribution to the poor benefits B. Such redistribution is under-supplied in an open economy, and so there is justification for redistributing to the poor—based not on a concern about the welfare of the poor, but rather about the welfare of the rich.

The non-poor may also benefit in other ways from providing income to the poor, such as a reduction in crime.

Secondly, some redistribution that occurs in the economy may be justified as insurance in circumstances where private insurance markets do not work well. A social safety net may be regarded as insurance against falling, for whatever reason, on hard times. Certain features of our social safety net, such as unemployment compensation, need-based transfers (such as food stamps and Medicaid), and retirement benefits (Social Security and Medicare) may be justified in part as an attempt to deal with failure of private insurance markets.

How Should Income in the Economy be Distributed?

It is possible to go beyond the issue of the provision of public goods (including redistribution) and ask a more general question: should income in society be redistributed to achieve a more equitable society—that is, a "just income distribution."

There are three basic philosophical approaches to the question of a just income distribution: the endowment approach, the utilitarian approach, and the egalitarian approach. There are also permutations of each approach.[7]

Endowment, Utilitarian, and Egalitarian Approaches

The *endowment approach* says that people should get what they earn. In its simplest form, it would imply no redistribution at all. Variations include allowing people to get what they earn in a competitive economy, so that excess profits arising from market power should be redistributed; to keep their labor earnings, so that assets and earnings from assets should be redistributed; or to keep what they would earn if they started equally in terms of wealth and family status. The last would, in theory, permit differences in income based on effort and willingness to take risk and innate earning ability, in contrast to the first approach that would also permit differences in income based on inherited wealth. Although the endowment philosophy does not support direct redistribution to yield a just society, the benefit principle is philosophically consistent with endowment notions of income redistribution and may support progressive taxation.

The endowment approach suggests there should be little or perhaps no redistribution, which is difficult to argue as a case of distributive justice. For example, it suggests that people with mental and physical disabilities that prevent them from working at a normal wage and who have no family to rely upon, should have little or no income. Given that people do have different innate physical endowments, many would argue that there is nothing especially fair about a system that allows individuals to have varied earnings based on inherited characteristics. At the same time, it seems unfair to penalize higher-income people who have those incomes because they worked harder or undertook more risk. On the whole, there may be a lot of support in our culture for allowing people to keep most of the fruits of their labor, but also a distaste for allowing individuals limited by circumstances of birth to suffer poverty.

The absolute lack of redistribution may also be inefficient, because of the presence of public goods in externalities in the real world, as discussed above. It means that everyone can be made better off, or not worse off, by allowing some redistribution.

The *utilitarian approach* says that society chooses to maximize welfare in the economy—a "greatest good for the greatest number" philosophy. The simplest utilitarian welfare measure is simply one that adds up all the welfare of the individuals in the economy and tries to make shifts that will make that welfare sum the greatest. Such an approach suggests that income should be shifted to those who are able to benefit the most from it at the margin.

This sort of assumption also implies an extremely progressive tax system in some circumstances: if we assume that all individuals are otherwise identical and that the value of each dollar of income declines as income rises (i.e., a dollar is more valuable to a poor man than to rich one), and ignore behavioral responses, then total welfare is greatest when all individuals incomes are equal. This redistribution would require a 100% tax on incomes above a certain level to be redistributed until everyone has the same income—a super-progressive tax system, with positive taxes at the top and negative taxes at the bottom.

Although the idea of the "greatest good for the greatest number" sounds attractive, its practical implementation is ambiguous, because there is no objective measure of "welfare" and no objective method of describing a maximum social welfare. The assumption of identical individuals may be a reasonable approximation for policymaking, but in reality individuals are not identical.

The third type of approach is the *egalitarian approach*, which says that everyone should be equally happy. In this case, the government would make transfers to the poor and also transfer more money to those who enjoy it less so as to raise their level of happiness. As with the case of the utilitarian measure, if one assumes all people are identical and that the value of an additional dollar of income falls as income rises, an aggressive redistribution scheme should be called for to equalize everyone's income. Both utilitarian and egalitarian welfare functions are consistent with the ability-to-pay principle.

A variation of the egalitarian approach that takes into account behavioral responses is called the "maximin" or "Rawlsian" criteria. With this approach, society redistributes so as to maximize the welfare of the poorest individual. With no behavioral responses, and identical enjoyments of income, society would again equate income by taxing away all income above the average and giving it to those below the average, but with behavioral response, a 100% marginal tax on the rich would not work because it would cause individuals to reduce their work effort. In the Rawlesian system one would raise the tax just high enough so that the revenue to be distributed was greatest. It has been argued that this approach would reflect the choices risk-averse individuals would make as a social contract if they had to decide on the distribution of income before they knew which position they would fill in society.

One of the problems with using a welfare function, such as the utilitarian function, which might be persuasive to people as a practical guide to dealing with income distribution, is that it does not take account of the possibility that income varies because people differ in their work effort and risk taking. Although many people might feel it is appropriate to redistribute income to lower-income individuals because they do not have the capabilities to earn a higher income, they are less likely to favor redistribution to people who earn less because they work less or because they do not work as hard as the average person.

Similarly, even if everyone were identical in wealth, and innate ability and work effort, incomes would vary if some people took more risks than others. Taxing away the returns to risky projects and providing a guaranteed cushion against any risk would make risk-taking irrelevant to economic decisions. As a result, individuals might be willing to take more or less risk than appropriate, and an optimal level of risk-taking is important to the efficient operation of an economy. Because differences in income that arise from innate capabilities or inherited wealth (whether financial and physical wealth, or human wealth provided by one's family) cannot easily be separated from those that arise from work effort and risk-taking, it is more difficult to assess the appropriate level of redistribution. Nevertheless, it is clear that appeals to a social welfare function do suggest that income redistribution may be appropriate. The U.S. tax system including all government layers actually engages in very little means-based redistribution, however.

What are the Implications for Tax Burden Distribution?

Unfortunately, these guidelines about redistribution and about rules for paying for government expenditures do not provide a concrete answer as to how the tax burden should be distributed. What is perhaps most interesting about the analysis is that certain social welfare philosophies that might seem compelling do potentially support progressive taxation, as does the benefit principle of charging for public goods. The ability to pay criteria for charging for public goods, while often invoked to support progressive taxes, however, provides little guidance without more information on individuals' preferences, unless the marginal equal sacrifice form is assumed.

It is also important to keep in mind that even if the federal tax is progressive, such progressivity may be needed to offset state and local taxes that tend to be regressive, in order to avoid an overall regressive U.S. tax system.

THE ESTIMATED DISTRIBUTION OF THE TAX BURDEN

Several public and private organizations have produced distributional tables. The governmental entities include the Treasury Department, the Congressional Budget Office (CBO), and Joint Committee on Taxation (JCT). Some of the private researchers involved in this work include the Urban Institute and Brookings Institution Tax Policy Center (TPC) and the Institute on Taxation and Economic Policy (ITEP) of Citizens for Tax Justice (CTJ).

Their analyses vary in several ways, including how they define income, the definition and ordering of tax units, and the taxes included. The following several sections discuss the rationale behind certain methodological choices and report the results of distributional analyses for different organizations, for different time periods, and for different kinds of taxes.

These measures are presented as effective tax rates, which makes comparison meaningful despite the methodological differences. The effective rates are simply the ratio of taxes paid to the income measure. They are different from the statutory marginal rates that apply to an extra dollar of taxable income only. When effective tax rates rise with income a tax system is progressive, it is proportional when effective tax rates are relatively constant, or regressive, if effective tax rates fall as income increases.

The Concept of Income

The theoretical discussion of the previous sections operated with a concept of "income," but what is the practical meaning of this word? There are several "incomes" mentioned in instructions to a single tax form—gross, adjusted gross, and taxable—to mention just three of them. Most states have state-specific income measures, such as "Wisconsin Income," usually different from the federal analogs. Other, non-tax, entities may use their own definitions of income better suited to their objectives.

Economic income encompassing all sources regardless of their taxability would be the best descriptor of the taxpayer's access to economic resources, but, unfortunately, none of the accounting or tax concepts of income exactly matches it. The discrepancy may happen for many reasons; one of them is statutory exclusions of certain items from income. For example, employees may have an option of purchasing their medical insurance through their employers with "pre-tax" dollars. "Pre-tax dollars" clearly represent income in the economic sense of this word, because employees can use them to consume, in this case—medical coverage. Yet they do not enter the calculation of "gross income" for individual income tax purposes, because of the special treatment of these transactions by law.

Organizations providing distributional analyses use measures of income that are expanded from tax measures, such as adjusted gross income (AGI). They estimate a more comprehensive income using various techniques. One of them, Treasury's Office of Tax Analysis (OTA), used Family Economic Income (FEI) as taxpayers' income measure in a 1999 paper.[8] The starting point of the intended income measure was the definition of income as the sum of consumption and the change in net-worth in a given period—commonly referred to as Haig-Simons income. This measure would include both cash and non-cash income, such as imputed rent on owner-occupied homes— the payments homeowners would have to make if they rented their dwellings instead of owning them.

OTA modified this definition in several ways. First, under the definition some retirees drawing largely on their savings would appear to have no or little income, because their consumption would be offset by a change in their net worth. At the same time, this money may be taxable, depending on the savings vehicle used. Their tax burden relative to their comprehensive income would appear extremely high because for several types of retirement accounts income is taxed on withdrawal. To correct for this mismatch, Treasury includes pension benefits in FEI. Another departure from the definition of income is exclusion of non-cash transfers, such as Medicare benefits, caused primarily by data limitations.

Other analyses use measures of income that may not be as broad as economic income, but broader than AGI. In its distributional table in 2003,[9] Treasury used a slightly narrower measure than in its 1999 study, cash income. CBO measures income as pretax cash income plus in-kind transfers.[10] JCT expanded AGI by adding tax-exempt interest, employer contributions for health plans and life insurance, employer share of FICA tax, worker's compensation, nontaxable social security benefits, insurance value of Medicare benefits, alternative minimum tax preference items, and excluded income of U.S. citizens living abroad.[11] The Brookings Urban Tax Policy Center initially used a narrower measure, but their current measures use both economic income and cash income. The choice of the income measure is influenced by data availability and other technical considerations as well as the types of taxes being distributed.

Using an expanded AGI or cash income measure is simpler and requires fewer assumptions, but it can mislead. For example, individuals may be accruing huge gains in assets, such as their houses, relative to their cash income. These problems with measuring income are reduced, however, when distributions are reported based on population shares (such as quintiles) rather than dollar amounts. On the other hand, dollar amounts lend a concreteness to a distribution table.

The overall tax burden measured as a share of AGI, or expanded AGI, would always appear higher than when measured as a share of comprehensive income. Also, any change in the distribution would appear to be more pronounced when measured as a percentage of AGI, because AGI would normally be lower than comprehensive income. For example, the comparison between AGI and FEI measures for 2000 shows that the former is smaller than the latter: $5,649 billion versus $8,419 billion.[12] This relationship between the two measures is likely to persist across time.

Some distributions may be reported based solely on AGI, which may be a good choice for a quick "back-of-an-envelope" analysis, but it is preferable to use more comprehensive income measures whenever technically feasible.

None of the organizations engaged in regular distributional analysis rely solely on AGI, however.

The measure of income can also affect impressions of tax burden unless distributional tables are presented based on population shares rather than measures of income.

Unit of Analysis

Another question facing the researchers is how to measure the unit of analysis, and also whether and how to account for differences in tax unit composition, especially when ordering data by population share (such as lowest quintile, second quintile, etc.). The unit may be the family, the household, or the taxpayer unit. In many cases, these units would be the same, but in others they would not. For example, an adult working child living in the parent's home may be part of the household, but would be a separate tax-filing unit.

In addressing unit composition, regardless of method of classification, issues arise with respect to ordering taxpayers. It is obvious that a large family may have more income than a single person, but still have the same ability to pay. Where is that family to be placed in ordering units for distributional analysis—with the same families by ability to pay or with the same by income but of different size? Researchers differ in their answers.

The first approach, used by most organizations, is not adjusting for the size of the unit at all. This approach can be argued to implicitly assume that income necessary to maintain a given standard of living for one person is the same as the one for four persons, which is certainly not realistic. Nevertheless, this approach is common. It is straightforward, eliminates some sources of ambiguity, and is the easiest to implement from a technical standpoint.

If households' positions in the income distribution are to be adjusted by family or household size, researchers must determine how to make adjustments. One possibility is dividing the burden by the number of persons, in other words conducting the analysis on a per capita basis. This approach fails to recognize the economies of scale larger tax units enjoy: buying a four-bedroom residence is usually less than twice as expensive as buying a two-bedroom unit. A price of a bedroom in the first case would be lower than in the second. In a way, the purchasing power of a dollar would be higher for a large household compared with a small one.

Several adjustment methods lie between these extremes. CBO orders households by ability to pay using this method: it divides income by the square root of the household's size.[13] In this case a four-person family would need to have twice as much income as a single taxpayer to be as well off.

Another methodology is to normalize income by expressing it in terms of the applicable poverty level. For example, if the poverty level for a single person is $9,000, and for a four-person family—$19,000, then a single taxpayer with $27,000 of income would be equated to the four-person family earning $57,000, because both of them would be making three times the poverty level for a household of the respective size.

These ordering procedures and unit measures probably do not make a great deal of difference in the overall qualitative pattern of the effective tax rates.

Incidence Assumptions

Another important factor in distributional analysis is the economic incidence of taxes. It reflects the notion that a tax burden is not necessarily borne by the taxpayers legally responsible for paying the tax. For example, imposing an excise tax may lead to a price increase. Thus, even though the seller would be legally responsible for paying the tax, the economic cost would be split between the sellers and the buyers in some way, possibly with the buyers bearing all of it.

Researchers have to make reasonable assumptions about incidence, because calculating the precise shares in every case is impossible. They depend on factors specific to every market segment and may fluctuate across segments and in time within every market. *Table 1* lists the assumptions about tax incidence incorporated in the models of OTA, CBO, JCT, and TPC.

Even though the variations in income, unit definition and incidence assumptions would cause the quantitative results to be different in every case, the implications about the tax system are actually quite similar.

The incidence of the corporate tax, in particular, has been the subject of a considerable economic literature, with the distributional effects depending on the responses of investors and workers and the technology of the firm.[14] The incidence of all taxes, even individual income and payroll taxes, depends, however, on behavioral responses. If savings and labor supply are relatively insensitive to taxes, as much evidence suggests, these taxes will fall on the individual who pays them.[15]

Table 1. Comparison of Tax Incidence Assumptions Used by OTA, CBO, JCT, and TPC

	OTA (1999)	CBO	JCT	TPC
Individual income tax	Payors	Payors	Payors	Payors
Employee's share of payroll tax	Payors	Payors	Payors	Payors
Employer's share of payroll tax	Families, for whom paid	Households, for whom paid	Taxpayers, for whom paid	Tax units, for whom paid
Excise taxes on final goods	Families, adjusting for the relative price effects, but allocated to income	Households, based on the consumption of taxable items	Households, based on the consumption of taxable items	NA
Excise taxes on intermediate goods (business purchases)	Families, allocated to capital and labor income	Households, allocated according to overall consumption	Households, according to overall consumption	NA
Corporate income tax	Families, allocated according to the share of capital income	Households, allocated according to the share of capital income	NA	Tax units, allocated according to the share of capital income
Estate and gift tax	Decedents	NA	NA	Decedents

Sources: Assumptions reflect Cronin, *U.S. Treasury Distributional Analysis Methodology;* Congressional Budget Office, *Effective Federal Tax Rates: 1979-2001* April 2004; Thomas A. Barthold, James R. Nunns, and Eric Toder, "A Comparison of Distributional Methodologies, in *Distributional Analysis of Tax Policy*, David Bradford, ed. (Washington, DC, The AEI Press) 1995, pp. 96-110, and personal contacts.

Note that the same assumptions about incidence are used (given the tax is distributed at all) for the different taxes except in the case of excise taxes. CBO and JCT allocate the tax based on the consumption of the taxed items. The Treasury allocates the tax to income, and also adjusts at the consumption level by imposing a burden for taxed items and a benefit for non-taxed items that nets to zero.[16]

Measures of Tax Burden Distribution

Current Federal Effective Tax Rates

Tables 2, 3 and 4 reproduce the burden distribution estimates from different sources for 2000, 2005 and 2006 ordered by population shares. Because of the methodological differences described above, the data are not precisely comparable. In addition, there is also timing discrepancy. TPC does not have a 2000 law distribution table using 2000 incomes, so the appropriate column uses 2004 incomes but 2000 law. OTA does not have the table for 2005. Note that the absolute measures of effective tax rates can be affected by the income measure and the composition of included taxes. *Table 4* differs from *Table 3* in that the tax rates are based on cash income for the TPC rather than economic income, and this difference results in much more similar tax rates.

At the same time, all sources depict a similar qualitative picture about the progressivity of the federal tax burden distribution. For example, in every case the effective tax rates for the lowest quintile are estimated in the low to middle single digits. The highest quintile in 2000 faced an effective rate of close to or above 25%. The numbers for other quintiles and the general pattern seem consistent, too. Tax rates rise more slowly, however, at the top of the distribution.

Table 5 and Table 6 present data from the Joint Committee on Taxation, reflecting the tax burden at 2003 levels of income, based on tax law prior to the 2003 tax cut and the tax burden in 2008 without incorporating the 2008 rebates. The tables are arrayed by income level rather than population proportion, but again present a very similar picture of the federal total effective tax rates.

Table 2. Tax Burden Distribution Estimates for 2000 by Different Research Organizations

	Effective Federal Tax Rates	Effective Federal Tax Rates (Excludes Estate Taxes)	Effective Tax Rates, 2004 Cash Income (Excludes Excise Taxes)
	OTA	CBO	TPC
Lowest Quintile	5.9	6.4	3.8
Second Quintile	11.7	13.0	9.3
Middle Quintile	17.4	16.7	16.0
Fourth Quintile	20.1	20.5	20.5
Highest Quintile	24.6	28.0	27.3

Table 3. Tax Burden Distribution Estimates for 2005 by Different Research Organizations

	Average Effective Federal Tax Rates Under Current Tax Law, (Excludes Estate Tax)	Average Effective Federal Tax Rates, Economic Income (Excludes Excise Taxes)
	CBO	TPC
Lowest Quintile	4.3	2.1
Second Quintile	9.9	7.1
Middle Quintile	14.2	13.5
Fourth Quintile	17.4	17.7
Highest Quintile	25.5	21.4
All	20.5	18.4
Top 10%	27.4	22.0
Top 5%	28.9	22.4
Top 1%	31.2	23.8

Sources: Congressional Budget Office, Urban Institute and Brookings Institution Tax Policy Center.

Table 4. Tax Burden Distribution Estimates for 2006 by Different Research Organizations

	Average Effective Federal Tax Rates Under Current Tax Law, (Excludes Estate Tax)	Average Effective Federal Tax Rates, Cash Income (Excludes Excise Taxes)
	CBO	TPC
Lowest Quintile	4.3	4.8
Second Quintile	10.2	10.9
Middle Quintile	14.2	16.7
Fourth Quintile	17.6	19.1
Highest Quintile	25.8	25.7
All	20.7	21.2
Top 10%	27.5	27.1
Top 5%	29.0	28.3
Top 1%	31.2	30.2

Sources: Congressional Budget Office, Urban Institute and Brookings Institution Tax Policy Center.

Table 5. Distribution of Taxes for 2003, Prior to the 2003 Tax Cut, JCT

Income Class (thousands of dollars)	Share of Population	Effective Federal Tax Rate (excludes corporate and estate taxes)
Less than 10	14.1	7.2
10-20	17.1	6.0
20-30	13.9	10.2
30-40	11.4	13.8
40-50	8.4	15.8
50-75	15.2	17.5
75-100	8.9	19.9
100-200	8.7	23.5
200 +	2.3	28.3
All	100.0	19.9

Sources: Data on population share from Joint Committee on Taxation, Estimates of Federal Tax Expenditures for Fiscal Years 2004-2008, JCS-8-03, December 22, 2003. Data on Effective Tax Rates, from CRS Report RL31907, *The 2003 Tax Cut: Proposals and Issues*, by David L. Brumbaugh and Don C. Richards.

Table 6. Distribution of Taxes for 2008, Prior to the 2008 Tax Rebate, JCT

Income Class (thousands of dollars)	Share of Population	Effective Federal Tax Rate (excludes corporate and estate taxes)
Less than 10	9.0	3.9
10-20	16.3	3.8
20-30	11.3	9.3
30-40	10.5	12.1
40-50	9.2	14.4
50-75	17.1	16.3
75-100	10.9	18.2
100-200	13.6	22.5
200 +	2.1	25.9
All	100.0	19.6

Source: Derived from Joint Committee on Taxation, JCX-14-08 http://www.jct.gov/x-14-08.pdf.

Burden Distribution of Different Kinds of Federal Taxes

The federal tax system contains two major types of taxes, payroll and income taxes, and two minor ones, excise and estate taxes. Income taxes can be divided into individual taxes that are applied to wage income, passive capital income (interest, dividends and capital gains), and profits of unincorporated businesses, along with a separate flat rate tax on corporate profits. Each kind of tax has a different degree of progressivity (or regressivity) and therefore, the distribution of the burden depends on the mix of taxes within the system. *Table 7* and *Table 8* show the distribution of the tax burden by type, before the 2001-2003 changes. *Table 7* reports the Treasury (1999) estimates and *Table 8* reports the CBO estimates, for all but the estate tax. *Table 9* reports the distribution for 2006.

The slight differences in the two 2000 distributions reflect differences in the income measures, in the taxes covered, and in the way in which families are ordered. For example, CBO places more larger families in the lowest quintile because they order by ability to pay, while Treasury orders by income. Since large families are likely to have larger benefits from the earned income credit, the tax rates of the individual tax are larger negatives in the CBO analysis than in the Treasury analysis. This effect also causes the lowest quintile to have higher payroll taxes because larger families are more likely and elderly individuals less likely to be represented in the CBO ordering.

The updated numbers in *Table 9* show similar patterns by tax types from CBO (data are not available from Treasury), but with some changes. Most significant is the income tax, whose burden is smaller at every level, but particularly at higher incomes, due to the 2001 tax cuts. Some effects are due to the shifting of income across the brackets as well, which reduces income (and effective tax rates) in the lower incomes and raises them in the higher ones. Without these incomes shifts, the tax cuts would be smaller in the higher brackets and larger in the lower ones. This effect due to income redistribution can be seen with the corporate tax, whose overall level rose due in part to cyclical factors, but whose burden at lower incomes fell.

Table 7. Effective Federal Tax Rates by the Type of Tax, 2000 (Treasury)

	Individual Income	Social Insurance	Corporate Income	Excise	Estate and Gift	Total Federal
Lowest Quintile	-2.4	2.3	0.9	0.7	0.0	5.9
Second Quintile	0.8	8.7	1.4	0.8	0.0	11.7
Middle Quintile	5.6	9.3	1.6	0.9	0.0	17.4
Fourth Quintile	7.8	9.8	1.6	0.9	0.0	20.1
Highest Quintile	13.7	6.7	2.8	0.9	0.0	24.6
All	10.1	7.9	2.3	0.9	0.5	21.5
Top 10%	15.4	5.5	3.3	0.9	0.7	25.7
Top 5%	16.9	4.1	3.8	0.9	0.9	26.6
Top 1%	20.2	2.1	4.6	0.9	1.3	29.1

Sources: Treasury, Cronin, et al.

Table 8. Effective Federal Tax Rates by the Type of Tax, 2000 (CBO)

	Individual Income	Social Insurance	Corporate Income	Excise	Total Federal
Lowest Quintile	-4.6	8.2	0.5	2.2	6.4
Second Quintile	1.5	9.4	0.6	1.4	13.0
Middle Quintile	5.0	9.6	1.0	1.2	16.7
Fourth Quintile	8.1	10.4	1.0	0.9	20.5
Highest Quintile	17.5	6.3	3.7	0.6	28.0
All	11.8	7.9	2.5	0.9	23.1
Top 10%	19.7	5.0	4.5	0.5	29.7
Top 5%	21.6	3.8	5.4	0.4	31.1
Top 1%	24.2	1.9	6.8	0.3	33.2

Source: Congressional Budget Office, *Effective Federal Tax Rates: 1979-2001*, April 2004.

Table 9. Effective Federal Tax Rates by the Type of Tax,2006 (CBO)

	Individual Income	Social Insurance	Corporate Income	Excise	Total Federal
Lowest Quintile	-6.6	8.5	0.5	1.9	4.3
Second Quintile	-0.8	9.2	0.6	1.2	10.2
Middle Quintile	3.0	9.4	0.8	0.9	14.2
Fourth Quintile	6.0	9.6	1.2	0.8	17.6
Highest Quintile	14.1	5.8	5.4	0.4	25.8
All	9.1	7.5	3.4	0.7	20.7
Top 10%	16.0	4.6	6.6	0.4	27.5
Top 5%	17.5	3.4	7.9	0.3	29.0
Top 1%	19.0	1.6	10.4	0.2	31.2

Source: Congressional Budget Office, *Historical Effective Federal Tax Rates:* December 2007.

Tables 7, 8, and 9 show that the degree of progressivity is very different among the types of federal taxes. The effective rate of the individual income tax rises from a negative tax in the lowest quintile to 20% or so for the top 1%. As noted earlier, the earned income credit can lead to subsidies at low levels.

Payroll, or social insurance, taxes rise slightly and then fall. This pattern occurs because the tax rate is flat with a dollar ceiling, but only applies to workers. Tax rates are lower at the bottom of the distribution because of the greater share of retired people, and are lower at the top because of the dollar ceiling. So the tax is regressive at the higher end of the distribution. Another important observation is that for the four bottom quintiles the effective rates of payroll taxes are higher than for the income tax.

Conversely, the effective rates of the corporate income tax increase with income from 0.9% to 2.8% in the Treasury analysis, from 0.5% to 3.7% in the CBO 2000 analysis, and from 0.4% to 4.9% in the CBO 2005 analysis. The rates are even higher for the top10%, top 5%, and top 1%. These rates are well below the statutory rates, because a relatively small share of taxpayers receive income from the source, and their tax payments are dispersed among all taxpayers in the class. The progressivity of the corporate tax is due not to the progressive tax structure, but to the allocation of capital income to higher-income individuals.

Excise taxes' effective rates vary markedly between the two research organizations, reflecting the allocation of the tax to factor incomes for the Treasury and to consumption for CBO. The Treasury analysis depicts this tax as largely proportional, while the CBO analysis shows it to be regressive. (The CBO approach, which is also used by JCT, is probably the more widely used in distributional analysis). The regressivity of consumption taxes under this incidence assumption occurs because consumption tends to decline with income.

The estate tax is the most progressive of all, although it is small. Since most estates are exempt or largely exempt from the estate tax, only relatively high-income people pay this tax. (The estate tax does not appear in *Table 8 and Table 9* because CBO does not include the estate and gift tax in its analysis.)

Distribution over Time

Another important issue is the change in the distribution in time. This issue is particularly relevant after the recent tax law changes of 2001-2003, but even in a more stable statutory environment the distribution evolves continually in response to economic and demographic developments. *Table 10* shows the historic effective rates for selected years made in December 2007.

The years shown include the first year that CBO provided such analysis, and years after major tax changes and economic changes (the 1981 tax cut phased in over three years, the 1986 tax reform phased in 1987-88, the 1993 tax increase, the year prior to the 2001 tax cuts, and the most recent year). Over this period, the tax system continued to be progressive, although overall taxes today are slightly lower than was typical earlier.

Table 10. Historical Effective Federal Tax Rates, Selected Years, 1979-2004 (Effective Federal Tax Rates for All Households)

	1979	1984	1988	1994	2000	2006
Lowest Quintile	8.0	10.2	8.5	6.6	6.4	4.3
Second Quintile	14.3	14.6	14.3	13.1	13.0	10.2
Middle Quintile	18.6	18.0	17.9	17.3	16.6	14.2
Fourth Quintile	21.2	20.4	20.6	20.4	20.5	17.6
Highest Quintile	27.5	24.3	25.6	27.4	28.0	25.8
All	22.2	21.0	21.8	22.3	23.0	20.7
Top 10%	29.6	25.2	26.7	29.4	29.6	27.5
Top 5%	31.8	26.1	27.8	31.3	31.0	29.0
Top 1%	37.0	28.2	26.7	35.8	33.0	31.2

Source: Congressional Budget Office, *Effective Federal Tax Rates: 1979-2006*, April 2009.

Table 11 examines the current and projected burden around the period of the recent tax changes and into the future. Tax rate cuts are still being phased in as one moves from 2004 to 2008, with 2008 the last year for the lower capital gains taxes and dividend taxes. The year that the original 2001 tax cut is fully phased in is 2010. As currently scheduled, none of the tax cuts would be effective in 2014. Note that effective tax rates are higher in 2014 than in 2000 because of real bracket creep—the failure to adjust the tax system parameters to the real income growth. It affects the lower quintiles most, while the legislative changes have benefitted the higher-income groups the most, and that effect would be more pronounced if the CBO burden tables included the estate tax, which, according to *Table 7,* accounted for 1.3% of income of the top 1% prior to recent tax changes.

The estimates in *Table 11* reflect current federal law; the actual pattern of tax changes will depend on whether and to what extent the 2001 and 2003 tax cuts are made permanent and what changes might be made to the alternative minimum tax, which, if it is not addressed, will eventually apply to a very large fraction of taxpayers, especially those with large families.

Table 11. Effective Federal Tax Rates in Select Years Before and After 2001-2003 Changes in the Tax Law

	2000	2004	2008	2010	2014
Lowest Quintile	6.4	5.2	5.8	5.8	8.3
Second Quintile	13.0	11.1	12.4	12.3	14.7
Middle Quintile	16.7	14.6	15.9	16.1	18.2
Fourth Quintile	20.5	18.5	20.1	20.5	22.4
Highest Quintile	28.0	23.8	26.4	27.1	28.8
All	23.1	19.6	21.7	22.1	24.1
Top 10%	29.7	24.9	28.0	28.5	30.3
Top 5%	31.1	25.6	29.3	29.7	31.6
Top 1%	33.2	26.7	31.2	31.2	33.6

State and Local Tax Burden

Consideration of the tax burden would be incomplete without taking into account the burden from state and local taxes. It is difficult to draw consistent comparisons among all states, because their public finance systems are different. ITEP calculated U.S. average effective combined state and local rates for non-elderly taxpayers. *Table 12* presents these results.

Table 12. State and Local Taxes in 2002, Shares of Family Income for Non-Elderly Taxpayers, U.S. Averages

	Effective Tax Rates (total taxes, before federal deduction offset)	Effective Tax Rates (total taxes, after federal deduction offset)
Lowest Quintile	11.4	11.4
Second Quintile	10.4	10.3
Middle Quintile	9.9	9.6
Fourth Quintile	9.4	8.8
Highest Quintile		
Next 15%	8.9	7.7
Next 4%	8.1	6.5
Top 1%	7.3	5.2

Source: Institute on Taxation and Economic Policy, Citizens for Tax Justice.

Table 12 demonstrates that the overall state and local taxation system is regressive, at least as far as non-elderly taxpayers are concerned. It is difficult to make broad generalizations, but the main reasons for the result may be a relative "flatness" of state and local income tax schedules, high reliance on sales and use taxes, and the relative importance of excise taxes. Both sales and excise taxes are regressive when allocated to consumption.

States and localities are not as flexible as the federal government in their ability to choose their tax structure, because they face competition from other states and localities. It is relatively easy to move from one state to another, and even easier to move across local jurisdictions. Large differences in tax rates would induce taxpayers, especially higher-income taxpayers, to move to states with lower taxes. Thus, one can argue that it is primarily the federal government's role to ensure that the overall burden distribution is progressive, if progressivity is desired.

The combined total U.S. tax system appears to be progressive but not steeply so, as regressive state and local taxes are combined with the progressive federal tax.

Lifetime Tax Burden

So far, discussion in this report has centered around the analysis of the tax burden at a single point in time, but there is an alternative view that cumulative lifetime tax burden is a better representation of the concept. Lifetime tax burden is simply the sum of all taxes paid each year during the lifetime. In most cases, individual income grows with time and then drops after retirement. That pattern means that the lowest percentile may include a very heterogeneous taxpayer mix: younger people still in school, retirees, and mid-career low-income earners.

From the policy perspective, each of these groups is different and bundling them together makes little practical sense. For example, a policy redistributing the tax burden from the higher to the lower quintiles may have different effect on a younger taxpayer and a retiree. It is conceivable that a younger taxpayer may welcome the policy, because of the lower tax on an anticipated higher future income. In the meantime, a retiree would be unambiguously worse off, because he or she has a small chance of benefitting from the lower future burden.

The issue of lifetime burden distribution is especially important in the analysis of intergenerational fairness, and in conjunction with national debt issues. The debt incurred today would have to be paid off in the future, meaning that the taxes of the future generations could be lower in its absence.

At the same time, the approach does not take into account the fact that a marginal unit of money is likely to have a higher value to the lower-income individuals than to the higher-income ones. Even though a younger taxpayer in the previous example may pay a lower aggregate lifetime tax bill, he or she might still prefer to pay less taxes when income is low rather than when it is high. So, in order to compensate the taxpayer for the reduction in his or her disposable income today, the increase in the disposable income in the future should be more than today's loss. Each taxpayer's rate of intertemporal substitution is different, and incorporating it into the analysis would add another hard-to-verify assumption.

Another reason that simple addition of tax liabilities throughout lifetime is not an ideal indicator is the time value of money principle. Under this principle, a dollar today is worth more than a dollar tomorrow. Although the complication can be circumvented in theoretical analysis, it may be another source of contention in the analysis of real-life events.

Nevertheless, examining tax burdens from a lifetime perspective is likely to reduce the progressivity of the tax system, as some of the progressivity observed in a single cross section reflects the tendency of individuals to have lower incomes in the early and later years of life.[17]

How to Measure Changes in Tax Distribution

Although it is straightforward to describe what makes a tax system regressive, proportional, or progressive, it is more difficult to characterize changes to an existing tax system. Indeed, it is difficult even to determine the degree of progressivity or regressivity of a system so that the old and new tax systems can be compared based on their degree of progressivity. Although a variety of progressivity indices and measures have been proposed, none has been entirely satisfactory and they can lead to different conclusions about relative progressivity.[18] This report will instead examine the measures that are often used to characterize tax changes.

Reports of the distributional effects of tax cuts sometimes appear to depict the same tax change very differently. This difference in how the cut is perceived for distributional purposes arises from the choice of distributional measure. Some of the measures that have been presented include (1) the share of taxpayers benefitted that fall below an income level; (2) the percentage reduction in taxes paid; (3) the tax cut as a percentage of income (both pre-tax and disposable); (4) the distribution of the tax cut by income class; and (5) the average tax cut. The first of these measures is most likely to tend to depict a tax change as favoring lower-income individuals relative to higher-income ones; the second measure is next most likely, and so forth.

An Illustrative Example

To illustrate this point, consider a 10% across-the-board income tax cut (all positive net tax liabilities reduced by 10%). Assuming that the bottom quintile of the distribution does not have tax liability, this tax cut could be described as one in which three quarters of the beneficiaries have cash income below $80,000, which might make the cut appear not to be particularly targeted to high-income individuals. Almost any tax cut that is a general one will benefit, in numbers, those outside the high-income taxpayers, because high-income taxpayers are, by definition, not very numerous. But this description of the tax cut does not reveal anything about how much of a tax cut different groups receive. *Table 13* illustrates how such quantitative measures of the types described above would look assuming everyone in each quintile and group has the same average income (an assumption that allows the calculation of measures in the lower brackets where some individuals have negative tax liability because of the earned income tax credit).

Based on percentage changes reported in the second column, the tax cut as a percentage of income tax liabilities, the tax cut may appear to be fairly equal across income classes (except for the lowest group). But that measure does not reveal very much about distribution, because people in the lower-income categories may have extremely small tax liabilities and a tiny change in tax could result in a very big percentage change. Expanding the measure to a percentage reduction in all taxes shows that a proportional cut in income taxes reduces total taxes proportionally more for high-income individuals. Even in this case, however, measuring the percentage reduction in tax liability has not demonstrated anything about the effect on income equality; it merely reveals that individual income taxes are more progressive than total taxes.

In discussing these measures that do relate to effects on income inequality, it is important to distinguish between absolute measures and relative measures. For example, average tax reductions per unit provide information on the absolute size of a tax benefit across the income classes, which is a straightforward measure, and is shown in the last column of *Table 13*. In this example, the second quintile has a tax cut of $21 per person and the highest quintile a cut of $2,841.

Table 13. Alternative Measures of Distribution for a Ten Percent Across-the-Board Rate Cut

	% Change Income Tax Liability	% Change Total Tax Liability	% Change Pre-Tax Income	% Change After-Tax Income	Share of Tax Cut (%)	Tax Cut Per Return ($)
Lowest Quintile	0.0	0.0	0.0	0.0	0.0	0
Second Quintile	-10.0	-0.7	0.1	0.1	0.6	21
Middle Quintile	-10.0	-3.1	0.6	0.7	7.0	259
Fourth Quintile	-10.0	-3.7	0.8	1.0	16.3	607
Highest Quintile	-10.0	-5.1	1.4	1.9	76.4	2,841
All	-10.0	-4.4	1.0	1.3	100.0	738
Top10%	-10.0	-5.5	1.5	2.1	61.4	4,562
Top5%	-10.0	-5.8	1.7	2.4	49.0	7,223
Top1%	-10.0	-6.2	2.0	3.0	29.5	20,991

Source: Calculated based on data from U.S. Treasury Distributional Analysis Methodology, by Julie-Anne Cronin, U.S. Department of Treasury, OTA Paper 85, September 1999. The term "Total Tax Liability" refers to all federal taxes plus state and local income taxes. The top of the first four quintiles is $17, $34, $59, and $100 thousand. Measured by cash income, the top of the first four quintiles is $16, $30, $50, and $80 thousand.

Another way of examining this same effect is to compare the distribution of the tax benefit with the distribution of the population in the first column of *Table 13.* If each taxpayer class is getting 20% (one-fifth) of the benefit, then the benefits are evenly distributed. But the 10% tax cut distributes benefits disproportionally to higher-income individuals, indicating that incomes are becoming more unequal on an absolute basis. Both of these measures can inform us about how a tax cut is changing income without being misleading, although it is important to remember that existing income and tax payments are more concentrated among high-income individuals. Thus, there is a tendency for absolute measures to show most across-the-board tax cuts as favoring higher-income individuals—because these individuals have a larger proportion of the income and pay an even larger fraction of the income tax. Moreover, unless a tax provision is refundable, it will have little benefit for the bottom fifth of the population.

A different type of measure is a relative one that tries to examine how the tax benefit is changing the overall relative distribution of income in the country—that is, is it making income shares more equal or less equal? In this case, a tax change that does not alter distribution provides tax benefits to different income classes in proportion to some measure of income. (Higher-income individuals would still receive high absolute tax cuts, but not higher tax cuts as a percentage of income.) In general, the best method for measuring this type of effect on inequality is to examine the percentage change in disposable (after-tax) income. If the percentage change is equal, then the tax change is not making incomes shares more equal or less equal. If the percentages are higher among higher-income individuals the change is making income shares less equal. Clearly, the across-the-board proportional tax cut is increasing inequality measured by the relative concept: incomes in the lower brackets are increased by considerably less than 1%, whereas incomes in the higher brackets are increased by 2% or more.

Illustrations from Recent Tax Legislation

These different measures have been used to report different tax cuts, sometimes with very different depictions, which are illustrated from distributional data provided for two recent individual tax cuts: the 2001 tax cut (originally H.R. 1836) and the 2003 tax cut (originally H.R. 2).

2001 Tax Cut

The 2001 tax cut was a multi-year phased in tax cut, which sunsets after 2010. *Tables 14, 15, and 16* provide data from the three sources we are aware of that provided distributional data for the 2001 tax cut. The first table presents data from the Joint Tax Committee for the latest year provided, 2006, when most provisions would be fully phased in. The percentage change in federal tax liability was reported directly. The percentage change in after-tax, or disposable, income, the measure suggested above as conceptually the best measure of changes in distribution, was derived from data in the JCT table.

As suggested in the previous section, the percentage change in federal tax liability shows the largest percentage changes at the lower income and the smaller ones at higher levels, except for the very top level. These numbers give the appearance of a tax cut favoring lower-income individuals. The numbers showing the percentage change in after-tax income suggest, however, that the largest benefit was in the highest income class. Both patterns show that benefits fell, and then rose at very high-income levels, but the percentage change in tax liability suggests the biggest benefits for the lower-income class, while the percentage change in after-tax income measure shows the biggest benefits for the top measure.

Table 14. Distributional Effects of the 2001 Tax Cut for 2006

Income Class (thousands of dollars)	Percentage Change in Federal Tax Liability, %	Percentage Change in After-Tax Income, %
Less than 10	-0.9	0.1
10-20	-13.6	1.1
20-30	-11.4	1.8
30-40	-7.9	1.5
40-50	-6.5	1.4
50-75	-6.0	1.4
75-100	-5.8	1.6
100-200	-5.1	1.6
200+	-6.1	2.4
Total	-6.1	1.8

Source: Column 2 is reported directly while column 3 is derived from Joint Committee on Taxation, Distributional Effects of the Conference Agreement for H.R. 1836, May 26, 2001, JCX-52-01. See Table 5 in the previous section for a notion of the shares of the population represented by their income measure; for example, the under $10 thousand group is about 14% of the population, while the over $200,000 group is about 2%. The table for 2006 did not provide the data to calculate that distribution.

Table 15 shows the percentage increase in after-tax income, based on data from CBO. CBO provided effective tax rates and distributional shares, but did not present any direct comparisons of the effects of tax changes; our distributional measures could be derived from their data, however. The effect of the 2001 tax cut is approximated by comparing 2010 and 2011, because the provisions of the 2002 and 2003 tax cuts that add to the 2001 cuts would be phased out before 2010. The analysis indicates that the largest percentage changes in after-tax income were received by the highest income classes.

Table 15. Percentage Change in After-Tax Income by Quintiles, 2001 Tax Changes Fully Phased in, at 2001 Income Levels

AGI Class	Percentage Change in After-Tax Income
Lowest Quintile	2.1%
Second Quintile	2.2%
Middle Quintile	1.8%
Fourth Quintile	1.6%
Highest Quintile	1.9%
All	1.9%
Top 10%	2.2%
Top 5%	2.6%
Top 1%	3.8%

Source: CRS calculations derived from data in Congressional Budget Office, Effective Federal Tax Rates Under Current Law, 2001, August 2004. The calculations compare 2010 and 2011.

Table 16 shows a distribution of the tax cut measure provided directly and a percentage of income that was derived from the Citizens for Tax Justice (CTJ) data. The CTJ measures are a percentage of pre-tax income rather than disposable income, which tends to make all percentages slightly smaller. In contrast with the JCT table, the CTJ data show fully phased-in taxes. Unlike both the JCT and the CBO data, it also included the effect of the cut in estate taxes, which was a significant part of the 2001 tax cut. The distribution of the tax cut shows, as expected, a very large share of the cut going to high-income individuals—almost 40% went to the top 1% of individuals. The tax cut as a percentage of income, a measure similar to the last column of Table 14, shows the lowest decile with the smallest amount, the broad middle receiving slightly less than average, and higher benefits in the top decline, particularly the top 1%—clearly showing a cut skewed to the rich. The larger effect for the top 1% as compared with Table 15 probably reflects the estate tax.

Table 16. Distributional Effects of the 2001 Tax Cut, Fully Phased in, at 2001 Income Levels

Income Class	Share of Cut, %	Percent of Income, %
Lowest Quintile	0.9	0.71
Second Quintile	5.3	1.82
Third Quintile	8.5	1.74
Fourth Quintile	14.5	1.82
Highest Quintile Next 15%	23.7	2.29
Next 4%	9.5	1.59
Top 1% Total	37.6 100	4.76 2.43

Sources: Citizens for Tax Justice and CRS calculations based on their data, as reported in CRS Report RL30973, *2001 Tax Cut: Description, Analysis, and Background*, by David L. Brumbaugh et al.

2003 Tax Cut

For the 2003 tax cut, the JCT did not produce a distributional table, but the Treasury Department did. CBO's effective tax rate tables cannot be used because they mix phase-ins from 2001 in the data. For the Treasury data, the only measure of distributional change presented (and no other could be derived from their data) was the percentage change in individual income taxes. Like the JCT, they present a percentage change in taxes, but unlike the JCT the change is confined to income taxes. Note that, unlike the analysis presented in their 1999 study, the income measure is cash income, rather than economic income.

The Treasury analysis, shown in *Table 17,* confronted a problem that illustrates the difficulty of reporting distributional effects through percentage change when the base can approach zero or become negative, as in the case with percentage change in income tax liability. The lower part of the income distribution actually had negative taxes, when refundable items such as the child credit and earned income credit were taken into account. Therefore, what Treasury actually reports for that class is a percentage increase in negative taxes; technically speaking (as a mathematical issue) the percentage increase should have been positive change, because negative taxes became larger. There is really no way to compare this number with the other changes; moreover, the class of under $30,000 probably accounts for almost half (about 40%) of the population. So it is difficult to know what to make of this analysis.

For the remaining classes, however, the measure appears to favor the lower-income individuals.

Table 17. Comparison of the Distribution of Total Individual Income Taxes, 2003

Cash Income Class	Distribution of Total Individual Income		Percent Change in Individual Income Taxes
	Prior Law	Law with 2003 Tax Cut	
less than $30,000	-2.0%	-2.6%	-15.5%
30,000 to 40,000	2.1%	1.9%	-19.3%
40,000 to 50,000	3.7%	3.6%	-14.0%
50,000 to 75,000	11.6%	11.7%	-11.1%
75,000 to 100,000	12.1%	12.0%	-12.7%
100,000 to 200,000	27.6%	27.9%	-11.0%
more than 200,000	44.8%	45.4%	-10.8%
Total	100.0%	100.0%	-11.9%

Source: Excerpt from a table prepared by the Department of the Treasury, released May 22, 2003.

A very different picture is presented with the distributional effect measured as a change in after tax income based on analysis by the Brookings-Urban Tax Policy Center (TPC), using the measure they favor, percentage change in after tax income. *Table 18 and Table 19* present this data for income classes and population shares. At that point, the TPC was using adjusted gross income as their income measure, although they later developed expanded income measures.

Among a variety of statistics released by the Urban-Brookings Tax Policy Center, one statistic presented is the average tax change among income quintiles. Their discussion cautions the reader in using this measure (as would the authors of this report), but it is included here for comparison purposes and to lend some concreteness to understanding the problem with percentage change in tax liability. As *Table 20* demonstrates, the average tax change in the lowest quintile, a group accounting for about half of the under $30,000 cash income group in the Treasury table, is only a dollar. Clearly, this group gained essentially nothing from the tax change. The entire under $30,000 group probably gained an average of about $20—again, a very negligible amount. Thus, while the Treasury table seems to suggest that this group benefitted more than average ("15%" as compared with an overall benefit of 11%), many people would not characterize the relative benefits in this way. The percentage change in after tax income, by contrast, suggests that these lower-income groups gained very little. It is particularly in these lower-income classes where average tax liabilities are small or negative, that percentage changes in tax liability can be highly misleading.

Table 18. Percentage Change in After-Tax Income from 2003 Tax Cut, Calendar Year 2003

Adjusted Gross Income (AGI)	Percentage Change in After-Tax Income
Less than $10,000	Less than 0.05%
10,000 to 20,000	0.3%
20,000 to 30,000	0.8%
30,000 to 40,000	1.0%
40,000 to 50,000	1.1%
50,000 to 75,000	1.2%
75,000 to 100,000	2.1%
100,000 to 200,000	2.2%
200,000 to 500,000	2.2%
500,000 to 1,000,000	3.5%
More than 1,000,000	4.4%
All	1.8%

Source: Urban-Brookings Tax Policy Center.

Table 19. Percentage Change in After-Tax Income by Percentiles, 2003

AGI Class	Percentage Change in After-Tax Income
Lowest Quintile	less than 0.05%
Second Quintile	0.3%
Middle Quintile	0.8%
Fourth Quintile	1.1%
Highest Quintile	
Next 10%	1.8%
Next 5%	2.3%
Next 4%	2.2%
Top 1%	3.6%
All	1.8%

Source: Urban-Brookings Tax Policy Center.

Table 20. Average Tax Change by Income Percentile, 2003

AGI Class	Average Tax Change
Lowest Quintile	-$1
Second Quintile	-$38
Middle Quintile	-$217
Fourth Quintile	-$482
Highest Quintile	
Next 10%	-$1,270
Next 5%	-$2,125
Next 4%	-$3,145
Top 1%	-$20,786
All	-$715

Source: Urban-Brookings Tax Policy Center.

ACKNOWLEDGMENT

This report was originally co-authored with Maxim Shvedov.

End Notes

[1] In theory, one can use a model to determine both the quantity of a public good and the share paid for by each individual, which is called a Lindahl equilibrium. See E. Lindahl, "Just Taxation—A Positive Solution," in *Classics in the Theory of Public Finance*, Richard Musgrave and A.T. Peacock, eds. (New York, St. Martin's Press), 1958.

[2] This follows from the fact that the income elasticity is the percentage change in quantity demanded divided by the percentage change in income, and the price elasticity is the percentage change in quantity demanded divided by the percentage change in price; hence the percentage change in price divided by the percentage change in income is the ratio of the income elasticity to the price elasticity.

[3] Theodore C. Bergstrom and Robert P. Goodman, "Private Demand for Public Goods," *American Economic Review*, vol. 63, June 1973, pp. 280-296; Theodore C. Bergstrom, Daniel L. Rubinfield, and Perry Shapiro, "Micro-Based Estimates of Demand functions for Local School Expenditures," *Econometrica*, vol. 50, September 1982, pp. 1183- 1205; Edward M. Gramlich and Daniel L. Rubinfield, "Micro Estimates of Public Spending Demand Functions and Tests of the Tiebout and Median-Voter Hypotheses," *Journal of Political Economy*, vol. 90, June, 1982, pp. 536-560.

[4] This information can be found on the World Bank website, at http://devdata.worldbank.org/external/dgsector.asp?W= 0&RMDK=110&SMDK=473892.

[5] For example, a utility function of the form $u = y^a$, where u is utility (an index of individual's welfare or "happiness"), y is income and a is a constant greater than zero and less than one,

would suggest a regressive tax structure if equal absolute sacrifice were used, a proportional tax structure if equal proportional sacrifice were used, and a progressive tax structure if equal marginal sacrifice were used.

[6] This argument was made in a famous economics article: Harold M. Hochman and James D. Rogers, "Pareto Optimal Redistribution," *American Economic Review*, vol. 59, September 1969, pp. 542-557.

[7] The discussion in this section can be found in public finance textbooks. See, for example, Richard and Peggy Musgrave, *Public Finance in Theory and Practice*, 5th ed. (New York: McGraw-Hill), 1989 and Harvey Rosen, *Public Finance*, 6th ed. (New York, McGraw-Hill Irwin), 2002.

[8] Julie-Anne Cronin, *U.S. Treasury Distributional Analysis Methodology,* U.S. Department of Treasury, Office of Tax Analysis, OTA Paper 85, September 1999, p. 7.

[9] This distributional table was issued as a press release on May 22, 2003 and examined the effects of the 2003 tax cut. It did not provide data, however, for measuring the effective tax rate, because it did not include a measure of income.

[10] Congressional Budget Office, Effective Federal Tax Rates Under Current Law, 2001 to 2014, August 2004, p. 2.

[11] See U.S. Congress, Joint Committee on Taxation, *Distribution of Certain Federal Tax Liabilities by income Class for Calendar Year 2001,* JCX-2-01, February 27, 2001, for details on methodology and pre-EGTRRA distribution tables for 2001, and CRS Report RL31907, *The 2003 Tax Cut: Proposals and Issues,* by David L. Brumbaugh and Don C. Richards, for the JCT's 2003 and 2008 estimates.

[12] Cronin, U.S. Treasury Distributional Analysis Methodology, p. 12.

[13] Roberton Williams, David Weiner, and Frank Sammartino, *Equivalence Scales, the Income Distribution, and Federal Taxes*, CBO Technical Paper 1999-2, October 1998.

[14] See CRS Report RL32517, Distributional Effects of Taxes on Corporate Profits, Investment Income, and Estates, by Jane G. Gravelle, and CRS Report RL34229, Corporate Tax Reform: Issues for Congress, by Jane G. Gravelle and Thomas L. Hungerford.

[15] Ibid., and also see CRS Report RL31949, *Issues in Dynamic Revenue Estimating*, by Jane G. Gravelle, for survey of the literature.

[16] The Treasury appeared to have adopted this methodology in order to keep the price level constant (consistent with their revenue estimating assumptions) and have the tax passed back to owners of factors of production (wages and capital) rather than forward to consumers. But allocating the tax to income is not the same as the actual theoretical incidence, however,—namely that the tax falls on wages and on the owners of capital existing at the time the tax is initially imposed (through a fall in value). It is not easy to convert this concept into an annual incidence measure, although the closest way to do so would appear to be to allocate it to consumption rather than income, because the burden is not realized until the asset is converted into consumption.

[17] A lifetime study of the total tax system found a close to proportional system. See Don Fullerton and Diane Rogers, *Who Bears the Lifetime Tax Burden?* (Washington, DC, The Brookings Institution) 1993.

[18] These indices and issues are summarized in Donald W. Kiefer, "Progressivity, measures of," in Joseph J. Cordes, Robert D. Ebel, and Jane G. Gravelle, eds., *The Encyclopedia of Taxation and Tax Policy*, ed. (Washington, D.C., The Urban Institute), 1999. See also Donald W. Kiefer, "Distributional Tax Progressivity Indexes," *National Tax Journal*, vol. 37, December 1984, pp. 497-513.

In: Tax Distribution and Revenue Analyses... ISBN: 978-1-61324-421-0
Editor: Anthony N. Treviso © 2011 Nova Science Publishers, Inc.

Chapter 2

INCOME INEQUALITY AND THE U.S. TAX SYSTEM*

Thomas L. Hungerford

SUMMARY

While the extent of income inequality is debated periodically, one rarely discussed aspect of inequality is its impact on the tax system. Given the nature of the U.S. federal tax system, changes in the distribution of income can have significant implications for who pays the taxes, how much they pay, and federal tax revenues.

One common measure to characterize inequality or the dispersion of income is the Gini coefficient, which varies from 0 to 1. A Gini coefficient of 0 indicates that income is evenly distributed among the population (that is, everyone has the same income) while a value of 1 indicates perfect income inequality (that is, one individual has all the income). Between 1980 and 2004, the Gini coefficient for household income increased from 0.403 to 0.466—a 15.6% increase. The Gini coefficient for earnings increased by 22.4% from 0.331 in 1980 to 0.405 by 2004. Inequality has, therefore, increased over the past 25 years.

The two major sources of federal tax revenues are the individual income tax and the Social Security payroll tax, accounting for almost 80% of total federal tax revenue. These two taxes have different tax bases, tax rates, and adjustments to income. Furthermore, the individual

* This is an edited, reformatted and augmented version of a Congressional Research Services publication, CRS Report for Congress RL34155, from www.crs.gov, dated January 6, 2009.

income tax system consists of the regular income tax and the parallel alternative minimum tax (AMT), which have different tax bases and tax rates. Consequently, changes in income and earnings inequality could have very different effects on different parts of the federal tax system.

Many of the parameters of the regular income tax are indexed to inflation. Nevertheless, with income growing faster than prices and with rising income inequality, more income falls into higher tax brackets. Individual income tax revenues as a percentage of GDP, however, do not appear to be associated with rising inequality because the income tax has become less progressive through legislative changes as inequality has increased. The parameters of the AMT, however, are not indexed at all. Consequently, the amount of income and the number of taxpayers subject to the AMT will increase dramatically over time because of income growth and rising income inequality in the absence of legislative changes. The actual increase in AMT taxpayers has been limited because of a series of enacted temporary "patches." Although the maximum taxable limit of the payroll tax is indexed for average earnings growth, rising earnings inequality has pushed more and more of covered earnings above the limit. Thus, the proportion of covered earnings that is taxable has fallen over the past 25 years.

INTRODUCTION

Public interest in issues of income inequality appears to wax and wane. Interest sometimes picks up at election time with a flurry of newspaper and magazine articles and opinion pieces. After the election, the issue often disappears from the public consciousness. While the extent of income inequality and income growth is debated periodically, one rarely discussed aspect of inequality is its impact on the tax system.

Arguments are offered for and against reducing income inequality. The classic argument against rising income inequality is the rich get richer and the poor get poorer. This can increase poverty, reduce well-being, and reduce social cohesion. Consequently, many argue that reducing income inequality may reduce various social ills. In contrast, there are those arguing that rising inequality is nothing to worry about and point out that average real income has been rising, so while the rich are getting richer, the poor are not necessarily getting poorer. In addition, many argue that some income inequality is necessary to encourage innovation and entrepreneurship—the possibility of large rewards and high income are incentives to bear the risks of innovation and entrepreneurship. Therefore, they assert the economic costs of reducing or eliminating income inequality may be high.

Some researchers are concerned about the consequences of rising income inequality. Research has demonstrated that large income and class disparities adversely affect health and economic well-being. Michael Marmot has studied health and social status disparities, concluding that health follows a social gradient—people higher in the social hierarchy tend to be in better health than people of lower status.[1] Richard Wilkinson provides evidence that high income inequality— large income disparities—and less social cohesion have a negative impact on the health of a country's citizens.[2] Robert Frank argues that even if all incomes are increasing and rising inequality is due solely to those at the top of the income distribution pulling away from the rest, the middle class can be hurt by the pressure to keep up with the upper class.[3]

Several factors have been identified as possibly contributing to increasing income inequality. Some researchers have suggested the decline in unionization and a falling real minimum wage as the primary causes.[4] Others have argued that rising returns to education and skill-biased technological change are the important factors explaining rising inequality.[5] Tax policy, especially the Tax Reform Act of 1986, has also been identified as a possible cause for rising income inequality.[6] Most analysts agree that the likely explanation for rising income inequality is due to skill-biased technological changes combined with a change in institutions and norms of which a falling minimum wage and declining unionization are a part.[7] Research suggests that tax policy, while possibly having short-term effects on inequality, does not have much impact on longer-term inequality trends.[8]

Given the nature of the U.S. federal tax system, changes in the distribution of income can have significant implications for who pays the taxes, how much they pay, and federal tax revenues. Furthermore, the tax system is one policy instrument used to change the distribution of economic well-being, which requires an understanding of how inequality affects the various components of the tax system and how the various components interact with each other. This report examines how income inequality interacts with the parameters of the U.S. tax system. The long-term trend in inequality and how this may be related to taxable income and tax revenues is examined. In addition, the implications of rising inequality for tax policy are investigated through illustrative tables.

TRENDS IN INEQUALITY

One common measure to characterize inequality or the dispersion of income is the Gini coefficient, which varies from 0 to 1. A Gini coefficient of 0 indicates that income is evenly distributed among the population (that is, everyone has the same income) while a value of 1 indicates perfect income inequality (that is, one individual has all the income). The 25-year trends of the Gini coefficient for household income and individual earnings are displayed in *Figure 1.*

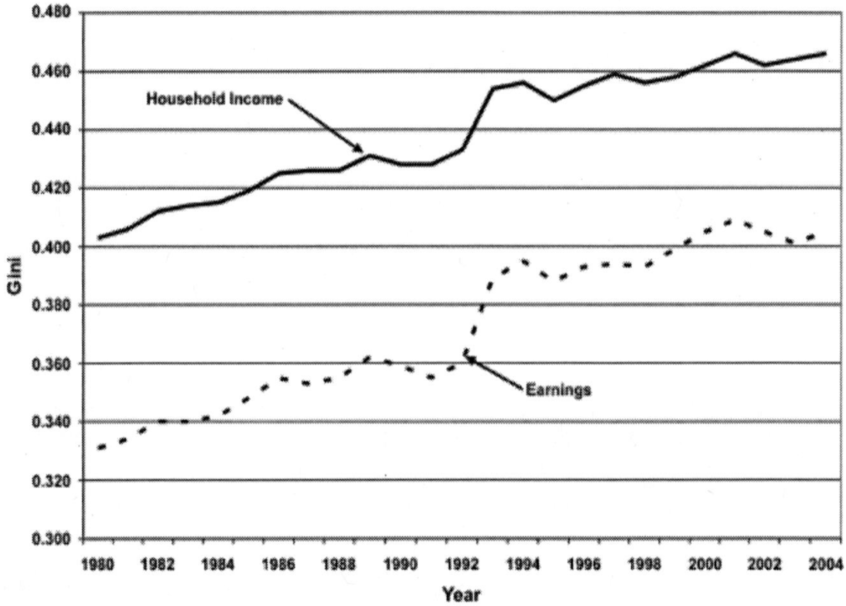

Source: Census Bureau.

Figure 1. Income and Earnings Inequality, 1980-2004.

Between 1980 and 2004, the Gini coefficient for household income increased from 0.403 to 0.466—a 15.6% increase (see the top solid line in *Figure 1*). For the most part, the Gini coefficient increased in each year. The earnings of full-time year-round workers also increased between 1980 and 2004. Although earnings inequality is lower than household income inequality (the dashed line in *Figure 1* is below the solid line), the Gini coefficient for earnings increased by 22.4% from 0.331 in 1980 to 0.405 by 2004. Earlier research shows that the Gini coefficient was fairly steady in the 1970s, and sharply increased beginning in 1980.[9]

Summary measures of inequality, such as the Gini coefficient, while useful in capturing overall changes in inequality, are less useful in locating where in the income distribution the changes are occurring. Consequently, more detailed information is required. Changes in the distribution of household income and earnings are examined separately.

Household Income

One direct method used to locate where in the distribution changes are occurring is to focus on income changes at various percentiles.[10] *Figure 2* displays the 25-year trends in real (inflation-adjusted) household income at the 10th percentile, median, and 90th percentile.[11] Real household income at the 10th percentile grew modestly by about 12% between 1980 and 2004 (increasing from $10,097 to $11,271) while median household income grew by 15% (increasing from $39,739 to $45,817). Real household income at the 90th percentile, however, increased by 36% over this period, reaching $124,908 by 2004. Household income at the 90th percentile was equal to 9.1 times household income at the 10th percentile in 1980; by 2004, it had reached 11.2 times household income at the 10th percentile. The increase in household income inequality between 1980 and 2004 thus arguably appears to be due to those at the top of the income distribution pulling away from the households lower down in the income distribution.

The next figure, *Figure 3*, provides a closer examination of the top 10% of the income distribution. The figure reports adjusted gross income (AGI), excluding capital gains, for various percentiles in the top 10% of taxpayers in the income distribution.[12] AGI at the 90th percentile increased by 15% over the 25-year period while AGI at the 99.5th percentile increased by 75% over this period. The evidence from *Figure 2* and *Figure 3* shows that the steady increase in income inequality since 1980 was due primarily to large income gains at the top of the distribution. The poor, however, were not getting poorer; their real income appears to have been roughly steady between 1980 and 2004.

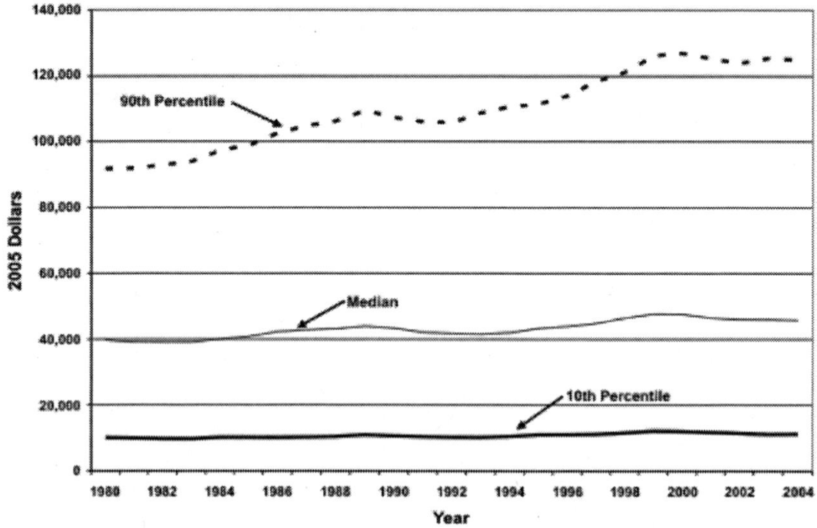

Source: Census Bureau.

Figure 2. Real Household Income at the 90 th Percentile, Median, and 10th Percentile.

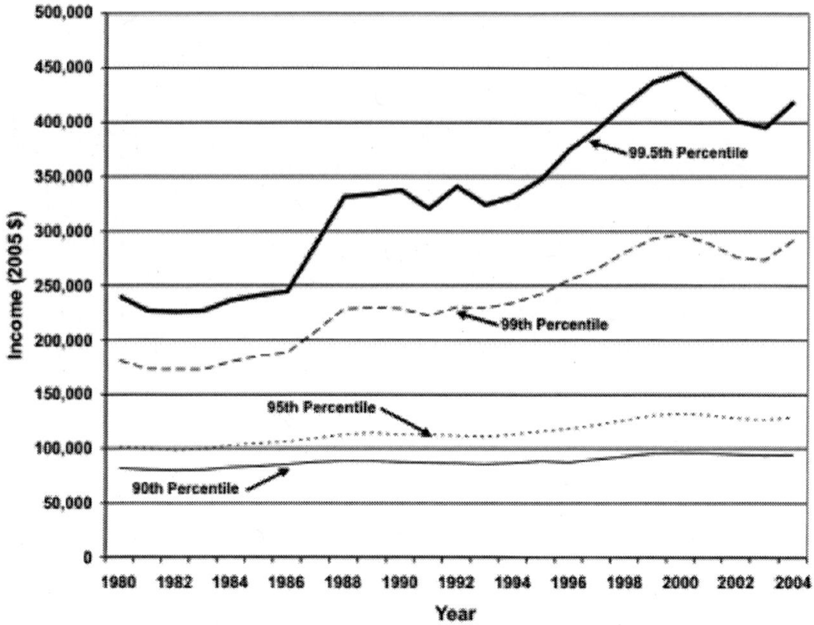

Source: Thomas Piketty and Emmanuel Saez.

Figure 3. Real Adjusted Gross Income of the Top 10% of Taxpayers.

Earnings

Earnings inequality in real terms increased dramatically between 1980 and 2004.[13] As with income inequality, the increase in earnings inequality was mainly due to those at the top of the earnings distribution pulling away from those lower down in the distribution (see *Figure 4* for the trend for men and *Figure 5* for the trend for women). While earnings inequality increased for both men and women, there are differences in how inequality increased between the sexes. On the one hand, for men, those at the top of the distribution pulled away from a largely static median and 10th percentile. The 90th percentile increased by 30% over the 25-year period, while the median grew by 1% and the 10th percentile fell by 4%. For women, on the other hand, the 90th percentile pulled away from an increasing median and 10th percentile. The 90th percentile increased by 58%, while the median increased by 27% and the 10th percentile grew by 7% between 1980 and 2004.

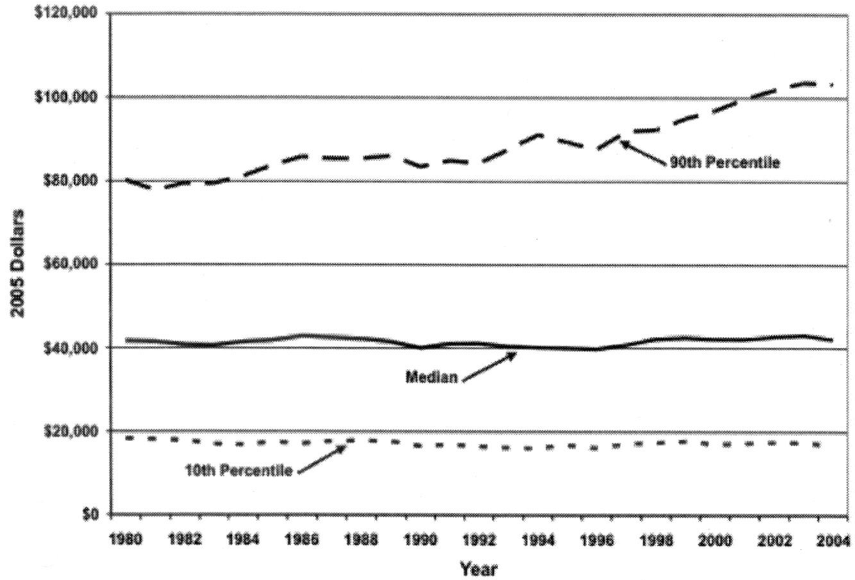

Source: Census Bureau.

Figure 4. Men's Real Earnings Inequality, 1980-2004.

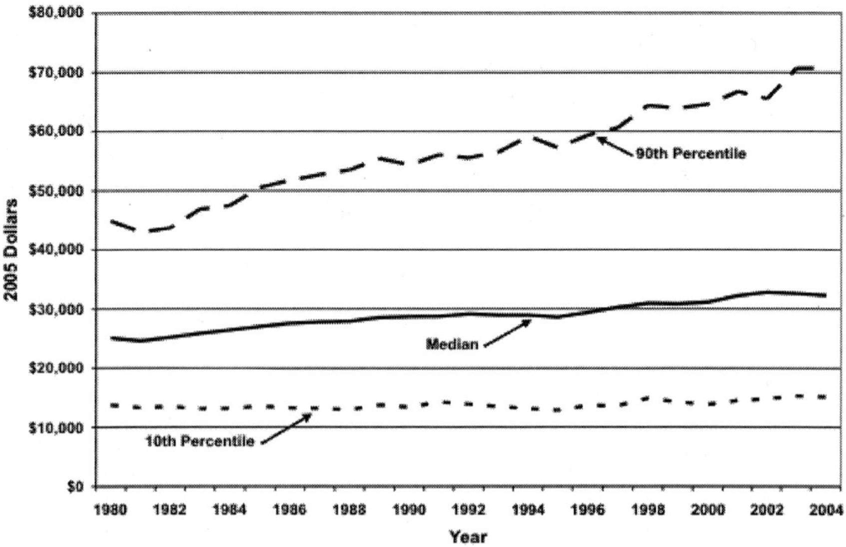

Source: Census Bureau.

Figure 5. Women's Real Earnings Inequality, 1980-2004.

TRENDS IN THE TAX BASE AND TAX REVENUES

The two major sources of federal tax revenues are the individual income tax and the Social Security payroll tax, accounting for almost 80% of total federal tax revenue. These two taxes have different tax bases, tax rates, and adjustments to income. Furthermore, the individual income tax system consists of the regular income tax and the parallel alternative minimum tax (AMT), which have different tax bases and tax rates. Consequently, changes in income and earnings inequality could have very different effects on different parts of the federal tax system.

The Regular Individual Income Tax

The tax base for the individual income tax consists of wages and salaries, tips, interest and dividend income, business income, realized capital gains, pension income, and other income.[14] The tax base is reduced by selected adjustments such as "above the line" deductions to produce adjusted gross income (AGI). AGI is reduced by exemptions (personal and dependent) and deductions (itemized or standard) to produce taxable income on which tax is assessed.

The U.S. federal regular income tax has a progressive rate structure with marginal tax rates increasing with income.[15] Gross tax liability can be reduced by various tax credits, such as the child tax credit and the earned income tax credit. Since 1984, personal exemptions, the standard deduction, and the tax brackets have been indexed to inflation, although they have also been periodically changed by legislation.

The ratio of taxable income to AGI has fluctuated somewhat since 1980 between a low of 65% and a high of 71% (see the solid line in *Figure 6*). Some of the fluctuations are due to the business cycle, to changes in tax law, and the increasing deferment of income through defined contribution pension plans (e.g., 401(k)s). Additionally, some the changes in this ratio could be due to changes in income inequality. The correlation between this ratio and the income Gini coefficient is 0.666, suggesting that as income inequality rises so does the proportion of AGI that is taxable.[16] Income tends to grow faster than prices over time; combining this income growth with rising income inequality suggests that over time more income will be above the personal exemption and standard deduction and, therefore, taxable. Consequently, although exemptions and the standard deduction are indexed to inflation, taxable income will grow with respect to AGI, holding other parameters of the tax system fixed.

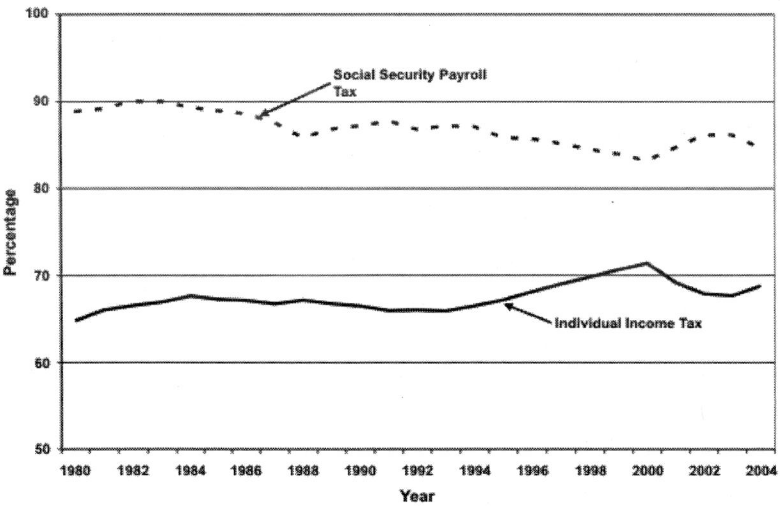

Source: Internal Revenue Service and Social Security Administration.

Figure 6. Ratio of Taxable to Total Income, 1980-2004.

Revenues from the individual income tax have also fluctuated over the past 25 years. The solid line in *Figure 7* displays the 25-year trend of individual income tax revenues as a percentage of gross domestic product (GDP). Most of the variation in revenues is due to the business cycle and tax law changes. Individual income tax revenues as a percentage of GDP fell in the early 1980s, the early 1990s, and 2001 because of recessions. Revenues increased in the 1990s due to tax increases and the long economic expansion with the latter having a more powerful effect. Revenues fell dramatically in the early 1980s because of the tax rate reductions enacted in 1980- 1983 and also fell after 2001 because of the 2001 and 2003 tax cuts. Increasing income inequality appears to have had little association with tax revenues—the estimated correlation between the Gini coefficient and the ratio of tax revenues to GDP is close to zero. Part of the explanation for this lack of association could be while rising income inequality has pushed more income into higher tax brackets, the top marginal tax rates have fallen over the past three decades. Recent research has shown that the regular income tax has become less progressive since 1960.[17]

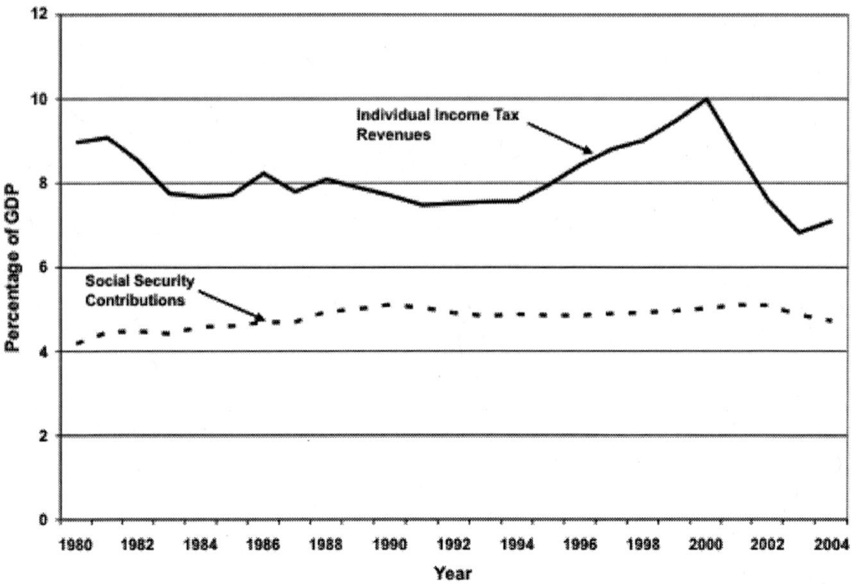

Source: IRS and SSA.

Figure 7. Tax Revenues as a Percentage of GDP.

The Social Security Payroll Tax

The Social Security payroll tax rate is 12.4%, half of which is paid by the employee and the other half paid by the employer (the self-employed are responsible for the entire amount).[18] The payroll tax has a constant tax rate, which applies only to covered earnings below the maximum taxable limit of $97,500 for 2007.[19] Covered earnings above the maximum taxable limit are not subject to the Social Security payroll tax. Since 1983, the maximum taxable limit has been automatically updated as annual average earnings increase.[20] The Social Security payroll tax rate increased periodically between 1980 (tax rate of 10.16%) and 1990, but has been steady at 12.4% since 1990.

Although the maximum taxable limit is indexed for growth in average earnings, the ratio of taxable earnings to covered earnings has fallen from 90% in 1983 to 85% in 2004 (see the dashed line in *Figure 6*). The estimated correlation between the ratio of taxable to covered earnings and the Gini coefficient is -0.860.[21] As earnings inequality has increased, a greater proportion of covered earnings falls above the maximum taxable limit and is thus not subject to the Social Security payroll tax.

Social Security contributions (tax revenues) as a percentage of GDP have varied between 4.2% and 5.1% since 1980 (see the dashed line in *Figure 7*). In 2004, contributions were equal to 4.7% of GDP. Although this ratio has not followed an upward trend like earnings inequality, the estimated correlation between the two is 0.676. It would appear that as earnings inequality increased since 1980, payroll tax revenues also increased, but not by much.

The Individual Alternative Minimum Tax (AMT)

The individual AMT operates parallel to the regular income tax. It has a broader tax base but a lower tax rate.[22] The original rationale for the AMT (and its predecessor) was to make sure high-income individuals paid at least a minimum of taxes. Higher income taxpayers calculate their regular tax liability and then their AMT tax liability; they pay whichever is greater.[23] Unlike the regular individual income tax, the parameters of the AMT are not indexed to inflation, but rather fixed in nominal terms. Consequently, over time the number of taxpayers subject to the AMT and AMT tax liability will increase due to income growth. While the AMT was established in its current form by the Tax Reform Act of 1986, Congress has made several changes to the AMT since then, recently enacting temporary "patches" so as to limit the number of taxpayers subject to the AMT.[24]

AMT tax revenue and the number of taxpayers affected by the AMT has fluctuated over the past 25 years, and has steadily increased since 1988 (see *Figure 8*). Both the proportion of taxpayers paying the AMT and the proportion of individual income tax revenues due to the AMT increased after 1982 with the enactment of the Tax Equity and Fiscal Responsibility Act of 1982, which expanded the individual AMT tax base. The Tax Reform Act of 1986 substantially modified the AMT by changing the tax rate and expanding the tax base, among other changes. The dramatic reduction in AMT taxpayers and tax revenues after 1986, however, was due to changes in the tax treatment of capital gains under the regular income tax. After 1986, capital gains income was fully taxed under the regular individual income tax and no longer taxed as a tax preference item under the AMT, thus reducing the number of taxpayers with capital gains income subject to the AMT.[25]

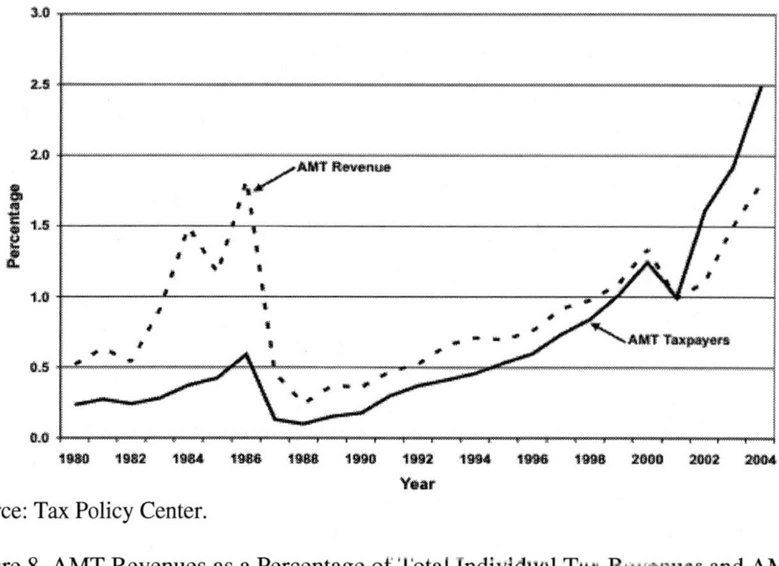

Source: Tax Policy Center.

Figure 8. AMT Revenues as a Percentage of Total Individual Tax Revenues and AMT Taxpayers as a Percentage of All Individual Taxpayers.

Both the number of AMT taxpayers and AMT tax revenue steadily increased after 1988 with a slight dip in 2001 due to the 2001 recession and tax changes in the Economic Growth and Tax Relief Reconciliation Act of 2001. Increasing income inequality since 1980 is correlated with AMT taxpayers as a percentage of all taxpayers; the estimated correlation is 0.714

and is statistically significant. The Gini coefficient, however, is not correlated with AMT revenues as a percentage of total income tax revenues (the estimated correlation is 0.339 and is not statistically significant).

IMPLICATIONS OF INEQUALITY FOR TAX POLICY

The regular individual income tax, the individual alternative minimum tax, and the payroll tax all have different tax bases and tax parameters. On the one hand, many of the parameters of the regular income tax and the payroll tax are annually updated for inflation and average earnings growth, respectively. On the other hand, the parameters of the AMT are not indexed at all. To illustrate how rising income and earnings inequality can interact with the various forms of indexation, the University of Michigan's Panel Study of Income Dynamics is employed.[26]

Table 1 shows the distribution of income among families in eight income categories for selected years between 1982 and 2004. The percentages displayed in the table show the share of aggregate total family income (realized capital gains are omitted from this measure) for all the families with annual income in the indicated income category or bracket. There are three scenarios:

- Scenario 1: the income bracket cutoffs remain fixed at the 1982 levels shown in the first column of the table.
- Scenario 2: the income bracket cutoffs are indexed to inflation in much the same way many of the regular individual income tax parameters are indexed. For example, by 2004, the cutoff for the first income bracket (denoted "Less than $10,000" in the table) had increased to $19,575.
- Scenario 3: the income bracket cutoffs are indexed to average earnings growth in much the same way the maximum taxable limit for the Social Security payroll tax is indexed. For example, the cutoff for the first income bracket had increased to $24,532 by 2004.

Panel A of *Table 1* shows how income shares have changed between 1982 and 2004 under scenario 1. The share of income to families in the first income category fell from 4.8% in 1982 to 0.6% by 2004.[27]

Table 1. Income Shares for Selected Years

1982 Income Categories	1982	1986	1990	1994	1998	2004
A. Fixed Income Ranges						
Less than $10,000	4.8	2.4	2.0	1.8	1.0	0.6
$10,000 to $19,999	14.5	9.4	7.4	5.9	3.9	2.7
$20,000 to $29,999	19.9	14.3	10.5	8.9	6.9	4.4
$30,000 to $44,999	25.4	22.4	17.3	15.7	11.6	8.6
$45,000 to $59,999	14.4	16.4	17.1	13.3	11.4	9.4
$60,000 to $79,999	9.6	13.3	4.0	15.8	13.3	11.9
$80,000 to $119,000	6.1	12.1	15.7	16.0	18.8	19.1
$120,000 or more	5.2	9.8	15.9	22.7	33.0	43.3
B. Income Ranges Keep Pace with Inflation						
Less than $10,000	4.8	3.3	4.1	4.5	3.3	3.5
$10,000 to $19,999	14.5	11.8	12.7	12.8	11.4	10.4
$20,000 to $29,999	19.9	17.2	15.8	15.7	13.6	12.4
$30,000 to $44,999	25.4	23.5	22.3	20.1	17.8	17.9
$45,000 to $59,999	14.4	16.0	14.5	13.4	13.9	13.1
$60,000 to $79,999	9.6	11.0	11.4	11.7	11.7	11.2
$80,000 to $119,000	6.1	9.2	9.4	8.3	10.6	10.9
$120,000 or more	5.2	7.8	9.9	13.5	17.7	20.6
C. Income Ranges Keep Pace with Income growth						
Less than $10,000	4.8	3.6	4.7	5.0	4.9	5.8
$10,000 to $19,999	14.5	13.3	14.0	14.1	14.3	14.3
$20,000 to $29,999	19.9	17.5	17.0	16.4	15.4	15.6
$30,000 to $44,999	25.4	24.9	23.4	20.6	19.2	19.2
$45,000 to $59,999	14.4	14.8	14.1	13.4	12.8	11.4
$60,000 to $79,999	9.6	10.4	10.4	10.4	10.6	8.9
$80,000 to $119,000	6.1	8.7	7.6	7.6	7.5	9.4
$120,000 or more	5.2	6.8	8.9	12.4	15.2	15.4

Source: Author's analysis of the PSID.

At the other end of the income distribution, the share of aggregate income received by those in the highest income category ($120,000 or more) increased from 5.2% to 43.3% between 1982 and 2004.[28] In general, income shifted from the lower-income categories to the higher-income categories between 1982 and 2004. Consequently, in the case of a tax system with fixed parameters, such as the AMT, more income and more taxpayers will be subject to the tax over time because of income growth and rising income inequality.

The income shares for selected years under scenario 2 (when the income category cutoffs are indexed to inflation) are shown in panel B of Table 1. Over time income tends to shift from the lower income categories to the higher income categories, but not to the same extent as when the category cutoffs are fixed in nominal terms (see panel A), since income tends to increase faster, on average, than prices over time. The percentage of aggregate income of families in the top income bracket more than tripled between 1982 and 2004, from 5.2% to 20.6%.[29] Even when tax parameters, such as exemptions and tax brackets for the regular income tax, are indexed to inflation, income growth and rising inequality will lead to more income being taxed and at higher marginal tax rates over time.

The results for scenario 3, with the income category cutoffs indexed to average earnings growth, are displayed in panel C of Table 1. Even under scenario 3, there is some evidence of income shifting up to higher income categories. Most of the shift, however, appears to be from the middle income categories toward the higher categories. The percentage of income in the bottom two categories remained fairly steady at about 20% between 1982 and 2004. The share of income of the next four categories ($20,000 up to $79,999) fell from about 70% in 1982 to 55% by 2004.

The share for the top two categories increased over this period from 11% to almost 25%, with the share of income received by families in the top income category increasing from 5.2% to 15.4%.

The distribution of individual earnings for the selected years under the three scenarios is reported in *Table 2*.[30] Although the earnings categories or brackets are different from the income categories in *Table 1*, the results reported in panel A are broadly similar to the results for family income. With inflation-indexed earnings bracket cutoffs, there is a general shifting of aggregate earnings toward the higher earnings categories over time (see panel B in *Table 2*).

Table 2. Earnings Shares for Selected Years

1982 Earnings Categories	1982	1986	1990	1994	1998	2004
A. Fixed Income Ranges						
Less than $10,000	11.4	7.1	5.3	3.7	2.9	2.1
$10,000 to $14,999	12.1	9.3	6.3	5.0	3.1	2.3
$15,000 to $19,999	14.4	10.4	8.9	6.4	4.6	3.0
$20,000 to $24,999	13.4	11.2	9.0	8.0	6.0	3.8
$25,000 to $29,999	11.9	11.4	9.9	8.8	6.3	5.0
$30,000 to $39,999	15.3	18.3	16.7	15.6	14.1	11.1
$40,000 to $54,999	10.3	13.7	18.3	16.2	17.5	14.9
$55,000 or more	11.3	18.6	25.6	36.3	45.5	57.9
B. Income Ranges Keep Pace with Inflation						
Less than $10,000	11.4	9.8	9.8	8.8	8.0	8.0
$10,000 to $14,999	12.1	12.1	12.2	10.4	9.8	9.5
$15,000 to $19,999	14.4	12.0	13.1	12.9	11.2	11.8
$20,000 to $24,999	13.4	13.1	12.1	11.5	12.6	9.9
$25,000 to $29,999	11.9	11.9	11.6	10.4	10.1	8.7
$30,000 to $39,999	15.3	16.1	15.3	14.4	12.2	11.1
$40,000 to $54,999	10.3	10.3	9.4	11.8	14.2	11.0
$55,000 or more	11.3	14.7	16.5	19.7	21.9	30.0
C. Income Ranges Keep Pace with Income growth						
Less than $10,000	11.4	10.2	11.2	9.8	10.6	12.2
$10,000 to $14,999	12.1	12.6	12.5	11.3	12.4	13.7
$15,000 to $19,999	14.4	13.2	14.0	14.1	14.0	13.3
$20,000 to $24,999	13.4	13.4	14.5	12.6	12.3	10.2
$25,000 to $29,999	11.9	12.1	9.9	9.2	8.6	7.0
$30,000 to $39,999	15.3	15.1	14.3	15.2	13.4	10.4
$40,000 to $54,999	10.3	10.0	8.6	9.6	11.3	8.7
$55,000 or more	11.3	13.5	15.1	18.2	17.4	24.4

Source: Author's analysis of the PSID.

The Social Security maximum taxable limit is indexed to average earnings growth. The final panel of *Table 2* (panel C) reports the distribution of earnings among the earnings categories under scenario 3 where the bracket cutoffs are indexed for average earnings growth. The proportion of earnings received by workers in the four lowest earnings categories remains almost the same between 1982 (51.3%) and 2004 (49.4%). The proportion received by workers in the next three categories fell from 37.5% in 1982 to 26.1% in 2004. Lastly, the share of aggregate earnings received by workers in the top earnings category increased from 11.3% in 1982 to 24.4% in 2004. Overall, the share of aggregate earnings received by workers with annual earnings above the maximum taxable limit increased from 29.5% to 38.2% between 1982 and 2004. Consequently, even indexing the maximum taxable limit to average earnings growth, the proportion of covered earnings that are taxable will fall when earnings inequality is rising.

CONCLUDING REMARKS

Income and earnings inequality have steadily increased since 1980. Research has demonstrated that rising inequality is due to those at the top of the income distribution pulling away from those lower down in the distribution—the rich are getting richer, but the poor appear to be holding their own. Since various federal taxes have different tax bases, tax rates, adjustments to income, and methods for updating the tax parameters over time, changing income inequality can have different effects on who pays the different taxes, and how much they pay. The two major components of the U.S. federal tax system are the individual income tax and the Social Security payroll tax. Additionally, the individual income tax system consists of the regular income tax and the alternative minimum tax (AMT).

In order to help protect taxpayers from bracket creep, many of the parameters of the regular income tax are indexed to inflation. Nevertheless, with income growing faster than prices and rising income inequality, more income is pushed into higher tax brackets. Individual income tax revenues as a percentage of GDP, however, do not appear to be associated with rising inequality, because the income tax has become less progressive as inequality has increased (that is, the top marginal tax rates have fallen).

The parameters of the AMT are not indexed, but rather are fixed in nominal terms. Consequently, the amount of income and the number of taxpayers subject to the AMT will increase dramatically over time because of income growth and rising income inequality in the absence of legislative changes. The actual increase in AMT taxpayers has been limited because of a series of enacted temporary "patches."

Although the maximum taxable limit of the payroll tax is indexed for average earnings growth, rising earnings inequality has pushed more and more of covered earnings above the limit. Thus, the proportion of covered earnings that is taxable has fallen over the past 25 years.

Rising income inequality can be ameliorated through the tax system and government transfers. Transfers to the poor and a progressive tax system can help limit rising inequality. But, given that the parameters of the various components of the tax systems differ, using the tax system to reverse rising inequality would argue in favor of a comprehensive understanding of how inequality affects the various components and how the various components interact with each other.

APPENDIX A. PARAMETERS FOR THE INDIVIDUAL INCOME TAX

Year	Personal Exemptions		Deductions as Percentage of AGI	Range of Tax Rates	Lowest Bracket	Highest Bracket
	Single	Married				
1980	$1,000	$2,000	22.6%	14.0%-70.0%	$3,400	$215,400
1981	1,000	2,000	22.6	13.825-69.125	3,400	215,400
1982	1,000	2,000	23.0	12.0-50.0	3,400	85,600
1983	1,000	2,000	23.1	11.0-50.0	3,400	109,400
1984	1,000	2,000	23.3	11.0-50.0	3,400	162,400
1985	1,040	2,080	24.1	11.0-50.0	3,540	169,020
1986	1,080	2,160	24.6	11.0-50.0	3,670	175,250
1987	1,900	3,800	21.9	11.0-38.5	3,000	90,000
1988	1,950	3,900	22.3	15.0-28.0	29,750	29,750
1989	2,000	4,000	22.7	15.0-28.0	30,950	30,950
1990	2,050	4,100	23.2	15.0-28.0	32,450	32,450
1991	2,150	4,300	23.6	15.0-31.0	34,000	82,150
1992	2,300	4,600	23.4	15.0-31.0	35,800	86,500
1993	2,350	4,700	23.4	15.0-39.6	36,900	250,000
1994	2,450	4,900	22.8	15.0-39.6	38,000	250,000
1995	2,500	5,000	22.5	15.0-39.6	39,000	256,500
1996	2,550	5,100	22.0	15.0-39.6	40,100	263,750
1997	2,650	5,300	21.4	15.0-39.6	41,200	271,050
1998	2,700	5,400	21.0	15.0-39.6	42,350	278,450

Year	Personal Exemptions		Deductions as Percentage of AGI	Range of Tax Rates	Lowest Bracket	Highest Bracket
1999	2,750	5,500	20.6	15.0-39.6	43,050	283,150
2000	2,800	5,600	20.3	15.0-39.6	43,850	288,350
2001	2,900	5,800	22.1	15.0-39.1	45,200	297,350
2002	3,000	6,000	23.0	10.0-38.6	12,000	307,050
2003	3,050	6,100	23.5	10.0-35.0	14,000	311,950
2004	3,100	6,200	23.0	10.0-35.0	14,300	319,100
2005	3,200	6,400	22.6	10.0-35.0	14,600	326,450

Appendix B. Distribution of Families

1982 Income Categories	1982	1986	1990	1994	1998	2004
A. Fixed Income Ranges						
Less than $10,000	24.4	19.5	16.3	16.4	12.3	9.4
$10,000 to $19,999	24.8	20.3	19.2	17.0	14.5	12.6
$20,000 to $29,999	20.2	18.5	16.4	15.4	14.9	12.2
$30,000 to $44,999	17.5	19.4	18.1	18.4	17.1	16.0
$45,000 to $59,999	7.0	10.2	12.6	11.1	12.0	12.3
$60,000 to $79,999	3.6	6.3	7.9	9.9	10.5	11.7
$80,000 to $119,000	1.6	4.1	6.4	7.2	10.7	13.4
$120,000 or more	0.8	1.6	3.1	4.5	8.1	12.4
B. Income Ranges Keep Pace with Inflation						
Less than $10,000	24.4	22.3	23.3	25.7	21.9	21.7
$10,000 to $19,999	24.8	22.6	24.4	24.2	24.7	22.9
$20,000 to $29,999	20.2	19.8	18.1	18.0	17.6	17.3
$30,000 to $44,999	17.5	18.1	17.1	15.6	15.6	15.9
$45,000 to $59,999	7.0	8.8	8.0	7.4	8.7	9.3
$60,000 to $79,999	3.6	4.5	4.8	4.9	5.5	5.8
$80,000 to $119,000	1.6	2.8	2.8	2.5	3.6	3.9
$120,000 or more	0.8	1.1	1.5	1.7	2.4	3.2

Appendix B. (Continued)

1982 Income Categories	1982	1986	1990	1994	1998	2004
C. Income Ranges Keep Pace with Income growth						
Less than $10,000	24.4	22.9	24.9	27.1	26.7	28.1
$10,000 to $19,999	24.8	24.3	25.3	25.4	26.7	25.6
$20,000 to $29,999	20.2	19.2	18.4	17.8	17.2	17.2
$30,000 to $44,999	17.5	18.3	16.9	15.0	14.3	14.5
$45,000 to $59,999	7.0	7.8	7.2	7.0	6.8	6.3
$60,000 to $79,999	3.6	4.1	4.0	4.1	4.3	3.7
$80,000 to $119,000	1.6	2.5	2.1	2.1	2.2	2.9
$120,000 or more	0.8	0.9	1.2	1.5	1.8	1.7

Source: Author's analysis of the PSID.

Appendix C. Distribution of Workers

1982 Earnings Categories	1982	1986	1990	1994	1998	2004
A. Fixed Income Ranges						
Less than $10,000	44.1	34.8	30.2	24.7	23.0	20.4
$10,000 to $14,999	15.1	14.8	12.1	11.3	8.5	8.0
$15,000 to $19,999	12.7	11.9	12.2	10.5	9.1	7.4
$20,000 to $24,999	9.2	9.9	9.5	10.2	9.1	7.3
$25,000 to $29,999	6.7	8.2	8.6	9.2	7.8	8.0
$30,000 to $39,999	7.0	10.5	11.6	12.9	13.8	13.9
$40,000 to $54,999	3.4	5.8	9.3	10.0	12.7	13.8
$55,000 or more	1.9	4.1	6.6	11.3	16.1	21.4
B. Income Ranges Keep Pace with Inflation						
Less than $10,000	44.1	39.7	39.4	36.2	35.8	35.6
$10,000 to $14,999	15.1	16.6	16.9	15.9	15.4	15.2
$15,000 to $19,999	12.7	11.8	12.8	14.1	12.6	13.8
$20,000 to $24,999	9.2	10.0	9.3	9.8	11.1	9.7
$25,000 to $29,999	6.7	7.4	7.3	7.3	7.2	6.9
$30,000 to $39,999	7.0	8.0	7.6	7.9	7.0	7.7
$40,000 to $54,999	3.4	3.8	3.5	4.9	6.1	5.2

1982 Earnings Categories	1982	1986	1990	1994	1998	2004
$55,000 or more	1.9	2.8	3.2	3.9	4.8	6.0
C. Income Ranges Keep Pace with Income growth						
Less than $10,000	44.1	40.4	41.6	38.0	40.5	42.8
$10,000 to $14,999	15.1	16.9	16.5	16.3	16.9	18.6
$15,000 to $19,999	12.7	12.5	13.1	14.6	13.7	13.2
$20,000 to $24,999	9.2	9.8	10.5	10.1	9.4	8.6
$25,000 to $29,999	6.7	7.3	5.8	6.1	5.4	4.4
$30,000 to $39,999	7.0	7.2	6.8	7.9	6.6	5.0
$40,000 to $54,999	3.4	3.5	3.0	3.7	4.2	3.8
$55,000 or more	1.9	2.4	2.8	3.4	3.3	3.7

Source: Author's analysis of the PSID.

End Notes

[1] Michael Marmot, The Status Syndrome: How Social Standing Affects Our Health and Longevity (New York: Henry Holt and Co., 2004).

[2] Richard G. Wilkinson, Unhealthy Societies: The Afflictions of Inequality (New York: Routledge, 1996).

[3] Robert Frank, Falling Behind: How Rising Inequality Hurts the Middle-Class (Berkeley, CA: University of California Press, 2007).

[4] See David S. Lee, "Wage Inequality in the United States During the 1980s: Rising Dispersion or Falling Minimum Wage?," Quarterly Journal of Economics, vol. 114, no. 3 (August 1999), pp. 977-1023; and John DiNardo, Nicole M. Fortin, and Thomas Lemieux, "Labor Market Institutions and the Distribution of Wages, 1973-1992: A Semiparametric Approach," Econometrica, vol. 64, no. 5 (September 1996), pp. 1001-1044.

[5] See John Bound and George Johnson, "Changes in the Structure of Wages in the 1980s: An Evaluation of Alternative Explanations," American Economic Review, vol. 82, no. 3 (January 1992), pp. 371-392; David H. Autor, Lawrence F. Katz, and Melissa S. Kearney, "The Polarization of the U.S. Labor Market," American Economic Review, papers and proceedings, vol. 96, no. 2 (May 2006), pp. 189-194; and Thomas Lemieux, "Postsecondary Education and Increasing Wage Inequality," American Economic Review, papers and proceedings, vol. 96, no. 2 (May 2006), pp. 195-199.

[6] See Daniel R. Feenberg and James M. Poterba, "Income Inequality and the Incomes of Very High-Income Taxpayers: Evidence from Tax Returns," in James M. Poterba, ed., Tax Policy and the Economy, vol. 7 (Cambridge, MA: MIT Press, 1993); and Roger H. Gordon and Joel B. Slemrod, "Are 'Real' Responses to Taxes Simply Income Shifting Between Corporate and Personal Tax Bases?," in Joel B. Slemrod, ed., Does Atlas Shrug? The Economic Consequences of Taxing the Rich (New York and Cambridge, MA: Russell Sage Foundation and Harvard University Press), pp. 240-280.

[7] See, for example, Frank Levy and Peter Temin, Inequality and Institutions in 20th Century America, National Bureau of Economic Research, Working Paper no. 13106, May 2007; and Autor, Katz, and Kearney.

[8] See Joel Slemrod and Jon M. Bakija, "Growing Inequality and Decreased Tax Progressivity," in Kevin A. Hassett and R. Glenn Hubbard, Inequality and Tax Policy (Washington, DC: AEI Press, 2001), pp. 192-226; Levy and Temin; Thomas Piketty and Emmanuel Saez, "Income Inequality in the United States, 1913-1998," Quarterly Journal of Economics, vol. 118, no. 1 (February 2003), pp. 1-39; and Edward M. Gramlich, Richard Kasten, and Frank Sammartino, "Growing Inequality in the 1980s: The Role of Federal Taxes and Cash Transfers," in Sheldon Danziger and Peter Gottschalk, eds., Uneven Tides: Rising Inequality in America (New York: Russell Sage Foundation, 1993), pp. 225-249.

[9] See Lynn A. Karoly, "Trends in Income Inequality: The Impact of, and Implications for, Tax Policy," in Joel Slemrod, ed., Tax Progressivity and Income Inequality (Cambridge, U.K.: Cambridge University Press, 1994), pp. 95-129.

[10] A percentile is a value indicating the percent of the distribution that is equal to or below it. Income at the 10th percentile, for example, is the income level such that 10% of U.S. households have income at or below this level.

[11] Household income includes all cash income received from public and private sources except realized capital gains. Realized capital gains are not annual income flow and are very volatile with large variations from year to year. Capital gains are not considered in this analysis.

[12] Adjusted gross income includes income potentially subject to tax. It includes wages, salaries, tips, dividends, business income, and income from some government programs (unemployment insurance and some Social Security benefits). Benefits from other government programs, such as Temporary Assistance to Needy Families and Supplemental Security Income, are not included in AGI. The unit of observation for tax data is the taxpayer rather than the household; there may be more than one taxpayer in a household.

[13] The unit of observation for earnings is the individual worker; individuals with no earnings are excluded.

[14] Not all interest and pension income is taxable. For more information on the individual income tax, see CRS Report RL32808, Overview of the Federal Tax System, by Jane G. Gravelle and Donald J. Marples.

[15] See Appendix A for the key parameters of the regular income tax since 1980.

[16] This correlation is statistically significant. The correlation between this ratio and the 90th-10th percentile ratio is 0.505. The estimated correlations do not control for other factors that may affect the taxable income-AGI ratio, and do not indicate causality.

[17] See James Alm, Fitzroy Lee, and Sally Wallace, "How Fair? Changes in Federal Income Taxation and the Distribution of Income, 1978 to 1998," Journal of Policy Analysis and Management, vol. 24, no. 1 (Spring 2005), pp. 5-22; and Thomas Piketty and Emmanuel Saez, How Progressive is the U.S. Federal Tax System? A Historical and International Perspective, National Bureau of Economic Research, Working Paper no. 12404, July 2006.

[18] For a more detailed description of the payroll tax, see Thomas L. Hungerford, "How Increasing the Payroll Tax Base Affects Tax Burdens," Tax Notes, vol. 115, no. 7 (May 14, 2007), pp. 643-648. Before 1984, the self-employed faced a tax rate that was lower than the combined employee and employer tax rate. Self-employed person can take an above the line deduction for one half of self-employment taxes they pay.

[19] Covered earnings are earnings from employment covered by the Social Security program. Covered earnings below the maximum taxable limit are called taxable earnings. See U.S.

Congressional Budget Office, Differences in Wage and Salary Income Included in Various Tax Bases, Background Paper, June 2005 for a discussion of differences in earned income used in various tax bases. The Medicare payroll tax is not considered in this report. The Medicare payroll rate is 2.90% and since 1994, there has been no taxable maximum limit for this payroll tax.

[20] The Social Security Trustees note that the real-wage differential (that is, the difference between the percentage change in the average wage minus the inflation rate) averaged 0.9 percentage point over the past 40 years. Consequently, average earnings have grown faster than inflation. See The Board of Trustees, Federal Old-Age and Survivors Insurance and Federal Disability Insurance Trust Funds, The 2007 Annual Report of the Board of Trustees of the, Federal Old-Age and Survivors Insurance and Federal Disability Insurance Trust Funds, April 27, 2007, p. 87.

[21] The estimated correlation is statistically significant. Similarly, the 90th-10th percentile ratio is negatively correlated (and statistically significant) with the taxable-to-covered-earnings ratio.

[22] See CRS Report RL30149, The Alternative Minimum Tax for Individuals, by Steven Maguire, and The Individual Alternative Minimum Tax: Historical Data and Projections, Tax Policy Center, November 2006 for detailed descriptions of the AMT.

[23] See CRS Report RL30149, The Alternative Minimum Tax for Individuals, by Steven Maguire for details on calculating AMT tax liability.

[24] The most recent patch to the AMT increased the AMT exemption amount for 2008. See CRS Report RS22909, The Alternative Minimum Tax for Individuals: Legislative Activity in the 110th Congress, by Steven Maguire and Jennifer Teefy for more details. The Tax Policy Center estimates that if the temporary changes for 2008 expire, then the number of taxpayers subject to the AMT will increase from 4.1 million to over 30 million in 2009.

[25] See CRS Report RL30149, The Alternative Minimum Tax for Individuals, by Steven Maguire.

[26] The Panel Study of Income Dynamics (PSID) is a nationally representative longitudinal data set of the U.S. population that has been ongoing since 1968. The replacement mechanism of the PSID for births is designed to yield a representative sample of the nonimmigrant population in each year. The PSID oversamples low-income households because it was created by combining the Survey of Economic Opportunity (SEO), a survey of low-income households, with a representative group of households from the Survey Research Center (SRC) national sampling frame. Consequently, family weights are used throughout the analysis. See Martha S. Hill, The Panel Study of Income Dynamics: A User's Guide (Newbury Park, CA: Sage Publications, 1992).

[27] The share of families in the lowest income category also fell from 24.4% in 1982 to 9.4% in 2004. See Appendix B for the distribution of families across the income categories for the selected years.

[28] The percentage of families in the top income category also increased from 0.8% to 12.4% between 1982 and 2004.

[29] The percentage of families in this bracket increased from 0.8% to 3.2%. See panel B in Appendix B. 30 Earnings includes wage and salary income and earnings from self-employment.

In: Tax Distribution and Revenue Analyses... ISBN: 978-1-61324-421-0
Editor: Anthony N. Treviso © 2011 Nova Science Publishers, Inc.

Chapter 3

SOURCES OF THE GROWTH AND DECLINE IN INDIVIDUAL INCOME TAX REVENUES SINCE 1994*

The Congress of the United States, Congressional Budget Office

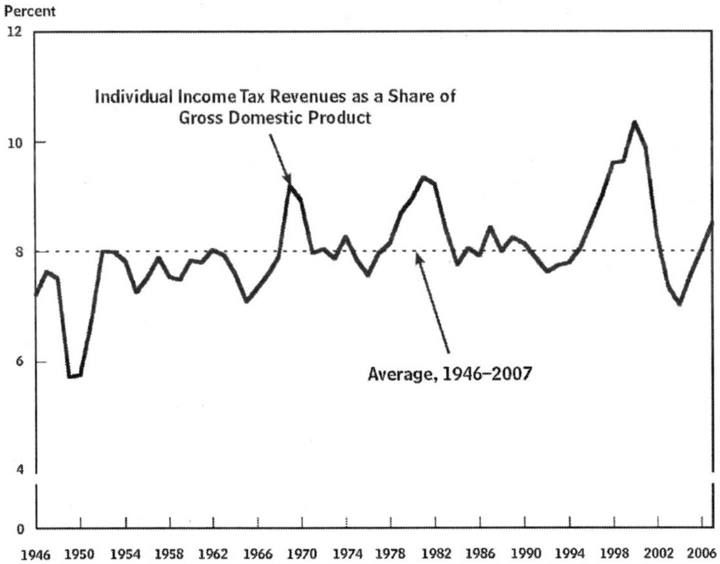

* This is an edited, reformatted and augmented version of a The Congress of the United States, Congressional Budget Office's publication No. 2221, dated May 2008.

PREFACE

Federal individual income tax revenues have risen and fallen by significant amounts since 1994. Although income tax revenues generally rise and fall with the economy, what is exceptional about the period since 1994 is the dramatic change in revenues relative to the nation's gross domestic product (GDP). The ratio of individual income tax revenues to GDP reached an all-time high in 2000, followed by a 50-year low in 2004. This Congressional Budget Office (CBO) paper explores the forces that have led to the rise and fall of individual income tax revenues relative to total economic output since 1994, expanding upon previous analyses in various editions of CBO's *The Budget and Economic Outlook.*

Kurt Seibert of CBO's Tax Analysis Division wrote the report with guidance from David Weiner, Frank Sammartino, Roberton Williams (formerly with CBO), and Tom Woodward. Doug Hamilton, Jonathan Huntley, and Arlene Holen (formerly with CBO) provided comments.

Sherry Snyder edited the paper, and Leah Mazade proofread it. Maureen Costantino prepared it for publication and designed the cover. Lenny Skutnik printed the initial copies, Linda Schimmel handled the print distribution, and Simone Thomas prepared the electronic version for CBO's Web site (www.cbo.gov).

Peter R. Orszag Director
May 2008

SUMMARY AND INTRODUCTION

Federal individual income tax revenues have risen and fallen by significant amounts since 1994. Revenues increased by $461 billion (85 percent) between fiscal years 1994 and 2000, fell by $211 billion (21 percent) between 2000 and 2003, and then increased by $370 billion (47 percent) between 2003 and 2007. Those changes in individual income tax revenues are partially responsible for a similar pattern in the overall budget balance.

Income tax revenues generally rise and fall with the economy, and changes in the level of economic activity explain some of the fluctuation in nominal revenues. What is remarkable about the period since 1994, however, is the dramatic change in revenues relative to the nation's gross domestic product (GDP). From 1994 to 2000, income tax revenues grew by 85 percent compared with growth of only 39 percent for nominal GDP. That growth increased the ratio of income taxes to GDP by 2.5 percentage points—from 7.8 percent to just over 10.3 percent, a historic high. In the following four years, that trend reversed, and individual income taxes dropped precipitously, falling to 7.0 percent of GDP by 2004, the lowest level in more than 50 years. Revenues rebounded in the next three years, rising to 8.5 percent of GDP by 2007.

Those changes in individual income tax revenues relative to the economy present a complicated story. The key factors include:

- A rising and falling income tax base, resulting from growth in wages and capital gains realizations that first exceeded and then lagged behind overall economic growth;
- A rising and falling effective tax rate on adjusted gross income, caused by changes in real (inflation-adjusted) bracket creep and a concentration of income in higher tax brackets; and
- Tax legislation, which was a major factor in the decline in income taxes relative to GDP from 2000 to 2004 but had little to do with the increase from 1994 to 2000.

Understanding those forces is critical to projecting the future path of federal revenues.

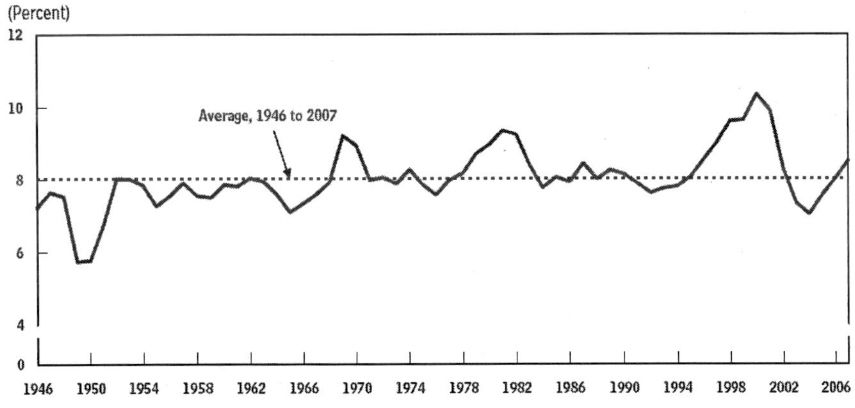

Source: Congressional Budget Office.

Figure 1. Individual Income Tax Revenues as a Share of Gross Domestic Product, Fiscal Years 1946 to 2007.

Historical Perspective

Income tax revenues ordinarily fluctuate as a percentage of GDP, but the magnitude of the rise and fall during the 1994–2004 period was exceptional. From 1946 to 2007, income tax revenues averaged just over 8 percent of GDP. Revenues have fluctuated around that average since 1946 but not by as much as the recent swings, aside from the years immediately following World War II (see Figure 1).

Previous revenue peaks occurred at the end of the 1960s and the beginning of the 1980s. Revenues reached 9.2 percent of GDP in 1969 following enactment of surtaxes during the Vietnam War era but fell in 1971 when those surtaxes expired. Revenues peaked again in 1981 at 9.3 percent of GDP as a result of high inflation and an income tax structure that was not indexed to inflation, causing more income to be taxed at higher rates. The 1981 tax cuts offset that rise and drove down the revenue share of GDP over the next few years. Troughs that occurred in the late 1940s and mid-1960s were caused by changes in tax law enacted during those periods.

Major Sources of Change from 1994 to 2004

This Congressional Budget Office (CBO) paper explores the forces that have led to the rise and fall of individual income tax revenues as a share of total economic output since 1994. The paper addresses changes in tax liabilities on a calendar year basis because the data needed to identify the sources of change are available only for tax liabilities that accrue in a calendar year, not for actual revenues collected in a fiscal year. (Fiscal year revenues are reported in the aggregate and are not identified with particular sources of income.) The pattern of change in calendar year liabilities closely follows, but does not mirror exactly, the pattern of change in revenues that occurs during the fiscal year, which starts and ends three months earlier than the calendar year.

This analysis focuses primarily on the 1994–2004 period because complete detailed data are not yet available for later calendar years. To assess the various sources of change in revenues, in this analysis CBO first adjusted the results to isolate the effects of legislation and then estimated how other sources of change contributed to the variations that would have occurred in the absence of legislation enacted after 1994.[1]

Changes in tax law accounted for little of the rise in federal income tax liabilities as a percentage of GDP between calendar years 1994 and 2000 but played a more prominent role in the decline between 2000 and 2004. In the absence of legislated changes, income tax liabilities would have grown by an estimated 2.7 percentage points as a share of GDP between 1994 and 2000—only slightly more than the actual growth of 2.4 percentage points (see Table 1). But between 2000 and 2004, that share would have fallen by an estimated 1.5 percentage points in the absence of legislated changes—about half of the actual decline.

Table 1. Sources of Change in Individual Income Tax Liabilities as a Share of Gross Domestic Product, Calendar Years 1994 to 2004

(Percentage points)			
	1994–2000	2000–2004	1994–2004
	Total Change in Income Tax		
Actual Changes (Including effects of legislation)	2.4	-2.9	-0.4
Changes Resulting from Legislation[a]	-0.2	-1.3	-1.6
Changes Excluding Effects of Legislation	2.7	-1.5	1.1
	Sources of Change		
Income Tax Base	1.5	-1.2	0.3
TPI growth more or less than GDP growth	0.5	-0.6	0
AGI growth more or less than TPI growth[b]	0.9	-0.6	0.3
Capital gains growth	0.7	-0.6	0.1
Other AGI growth	0.2	0	0.2
Effective Tax Rate on AGI[c]	1.2	-0.3	0.9
Per capita TPI growth more or less than inflation	0.8	-0.3	0.5
Income distribution and other factors	0.4	-0.1	0.4

Source: Congressional Budget Office using data from the Internal Revenue Service's Statistics of Income. Note: TPI = taxable personal income; GDP = gross domestic product; AGI = adjusted gross income.

[a] Excludes capital gains liabilities.

[b] Adjusted gross income has been modified to remove the impact of legislation since 1994.

[c] Excludes capital gains.

Excluding the effects of legislation, most of the variation in income tax receipts relative to GDP resulted from three factors:

- Fluctuations in taxable personal income relative to total economic output,
- Changing amounts of capital gains liabilities, and
- Changes in the effective individual tax rate.

A significant portion of the rise and fall of income taxes relative to GDP was the result of fluctuations in the size of the income tax base relative to total economic output. Growth in wages and other taxable personal income outpaced overall economic growth between 1994 and 2000 and was responsible for 20 percent of the 2.7-percentagepoint increase in the income tax share of GDP that would have occurred in the absence of legislation (see Figure 2). Wages grew more slowly than GDP over the 2000–2004 period, offsetting all of the excess growth from the earlier period. The slower growth in wages and other components of taxable personal income accounted for about 37 percent of the 1.5-percentage-point decline that would have occurred in the absence of tax legislation between 2000 and 2004.

Changing amounts of capital gains liabilities also played an important role in explaining why individual income liabilities rose and then fell relative to GDP. The ratio of capital gains liabilities to GDP increased from 0.5 percent in 1994 to 1.3 percent in 2000, accounting for about 28 percent of the increase in the tax share of GDP in the absence of legislation. In contrast, between 2000 and 2004 the ratio of capital gains liabilities to GDP declined from 1.3 percent to 0.6 percent, accounting for about 42 percent of the total decline in income tax liabilities that would have occurred in the absence of legislation.

Changes in the effective individual income tax rate—the ratio of income taxes to adjusted gross income (AGI)— accounted for almost all of the remaining change in the ratio of income taxes to GDP. A number of factors can cause the effective rate to rise or fall, including real growth in per capita income, which pushes more income into higher tax brackets (real bracket creep), and changes in the distribution of income, which can increase or decrease the concentration of income in the highest income tax brackets. Between 1994 and 2000, changes in the effective tax rate accounted for almost 45 percent of the 2.7-percentage-point rise in the ratio of liabilities to GDP that would have occurred in the absence of legislation; from 2000 to 2004, they accounted for about 21 percent of the 1.5-percentage-point decline that would have occurred without new tax legislation.

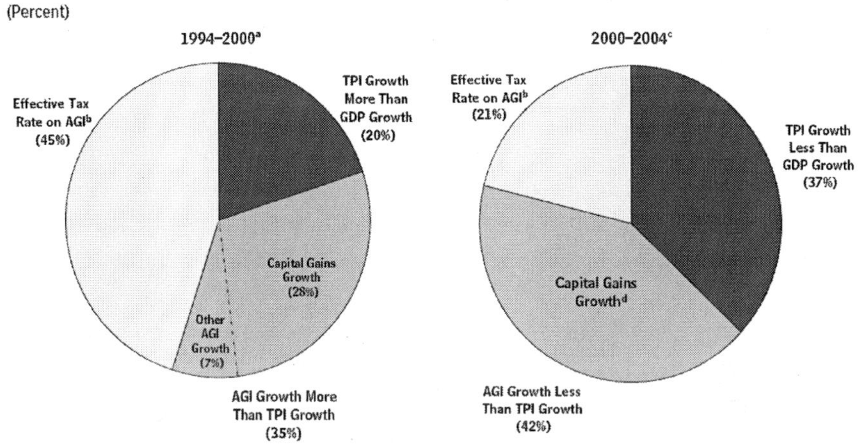

Source: Congressional Budget Office using data from the Internal Revenue Service's Statistics of Income. Note: TPI = taxable personal income; GDP = gross domestic product; AGI = adjusted gross income.

[a] The ratio of liabilities to GDP rose 2.7 percentage points from 1994 to 2000.

[b] Excludes capital gains.

[c] The ratio of liabilities to GDP fell 1.5 percentage points from 2000 to 2004.

[d] Growth in capital gains liabilities accounted for almost all of the growth in AGI; the amount attributed to other growth in AGI rounds to zero.

Figure 2. Contribution of Various Sources to the Change in Individual Income Tax Liabilities as a Share of Gross Domestic Product, Calendar Years 1994 to 2004.

CAUSES OF CHANGES IN INDIVIDUAL INCOME TAX REVENUES, 1994 TO 2004

Decomposing the changes in individual income tax revenues into the various sources can help explain the rise and fall and subsequent rise of revenues since 1994. The analysis focuses on the fluctuations in revenues as a share of GDP from 1994 to 2004. A later section of this paper presents a preliminary analysis of factors underlying the rise in that share of GDP from 2004 to 2007.

This analysis uses data from the Internal Revenue Service's Statistics of Income (SOI) sample for each calendar year from 1994 to 2004. The estimates based on SOI data differ from those based on fiscal year collections in several ways. First, they are based on taxes owed for a particular calendar year, not on taxes paid (or collected) in a fiscal year. Thus, "income tax liabilities from

2002" refers to income taxes owed on all income accrued during 2002, not all income taxes collected by the government between October 1, 2001, and September 30, 2002. In most years, between 70 percent and 80 percent of individual income tax liabilities for the calendar year are collected in the same fiscal year through withholding and quarterly estimated payments, but a very high percentage of taxes on volatile sources of income, such as capital gains and bonuses, is collected in the fiscal year following the calendar year in which those liabilities accrue. That timing explains why the trough in calendar year liabilities as a percentage of GDP occurred in 2003 but the trough in fiscal year revenues occurred in 2004. Second, the SOI sample is drawn only from individual income tax returns and thus excludes some income taxes paid by estates and trusts.[2] Finally, the sample for each year contains some returns from prior years.

Individual income tax liabilities grew from 7.6 percent of GDP in calendar year 1994 to 10.0 percent in 2000, an increase of 2.4 percentage points. Liabilities dropped to 6.7 percent of GDP in 2003 before rising slightly to 7.1 percent in 2004, a net decline of 2.9 percentage points. That sharp rise and fall follows the same general pattern as the change in fiscal year revenues.

Three factors were primarily responsible for the rise and fall of liabilities relative to total economic output:

- Legislative changes,
- A rising and falling income tax base (measured as the ratio of taxable income to GDP), including changing amounts of capital gains liabilities, and
- Changes in the effective individual income tax rate.

The following sections explore each of these factors in turn.

Legislative Changes

Several major pieces of legislation—the Taxpayer Relief Act of 1997, the Economic Growth and Tax Relief Reconciliation Act of 2001 (EGTRRA), and the Jobs and Growth Tax Relief Reconciliation Act of 2003 (JGTRRA)—all lowered individual income tax liabilities between 1994 and 2004. Other tax legislation enacted in that period did not have a significant effect on liabilities.

Legislation accounted for little of the change in income tax liabilities as a percentage of GDP between 1994 and 2000 but was a much more important factor in the decline in that share between 2000 and 2004. The Taxpayer Relief Act of 1997, which reduced income taxes, lowered the ratio of individual income tax liabilities to GDP by an estimated 0.2 percentage points between 1994 and 2000 (see Table 1). Over the next four years, however, that ratio fell by an estimated 1.3 percentage points, primarily because of the effects of EGTRRA and JGTRRA. That drop represents almost half of the total decline over the 2000–2004 period. In the absence of legislated changes, liabilities as a share of GDP would have grown by an estimated 2.7 percentage points between 1994 and 2000, only slightly more than the actual growth (2.4 percentage points), but would have fallen by 1.5 percentage points between 2000 and 2004.

The estimated effects of legislation reported here exclude the following:

- The impact of legislation on capital gains liabilities,
- The impact of tax changes on the amount of income reported on tax returns, and
- Any potential feedback effect of the tax changes on the economy.

These estimates exclude the *impact of legislation on capital gains liabilities.* Because gains can easily be shifted in response to legislation as taxpayers attempt to realize gains when tax rates are low, behavioral effects cannot easily be separated from other effects. Moreover, how taxpayers will actually respond to changes in the taxation of capital gains is highly uncertain.

The estimated effect of legislation also excludes *the impact of tax changes on the amount of income reported on tax returns.* For example, lowering tax rates could reduce the incentive for people to shift income into tax-deferred accounts, such as 401(k) retirement plans. That type of income shifting is not observed in the data, however, because the analysis is based on the actual income reported on tax forms and the amount of income that would have been reported in the absence of legislation is not known. In addition, although the model that CBO used to estimate liabilities captures almost all of the legislative effects between 1994 and 2004, some changes in legislation were too small or too complex to be included.

One check on the estimates of legislative effects on calendar year liabilities is to see how closely they track CBO's estimates of legislative effects on fiscal year revenues (see Figure 3).[3] The latter estimates include the impact of legislation on capital gains revenues, the type of income shifting omitted in the estimates of calendar year liabilities, and the effects of legislative changes too small or complex to be included in CBO's calendar year liability estimates. Thus, comparing the two sets of estimates highlights the effect those limitations have on the estimates of calendar year liabilities used in this analysis. Generally, the estimates of liabilities are close to those of fiscal year revenues. For example, legislation is estimated to have reduced income tax revenues by 12 percent, 18 percent, and 24 percent for 2002, 2003, and 2004, respectively, compared with estimated reductions in calendar year liabilities, as calculated for this analysis, of 11 percent, 19 percent, and 18 percent.[4]

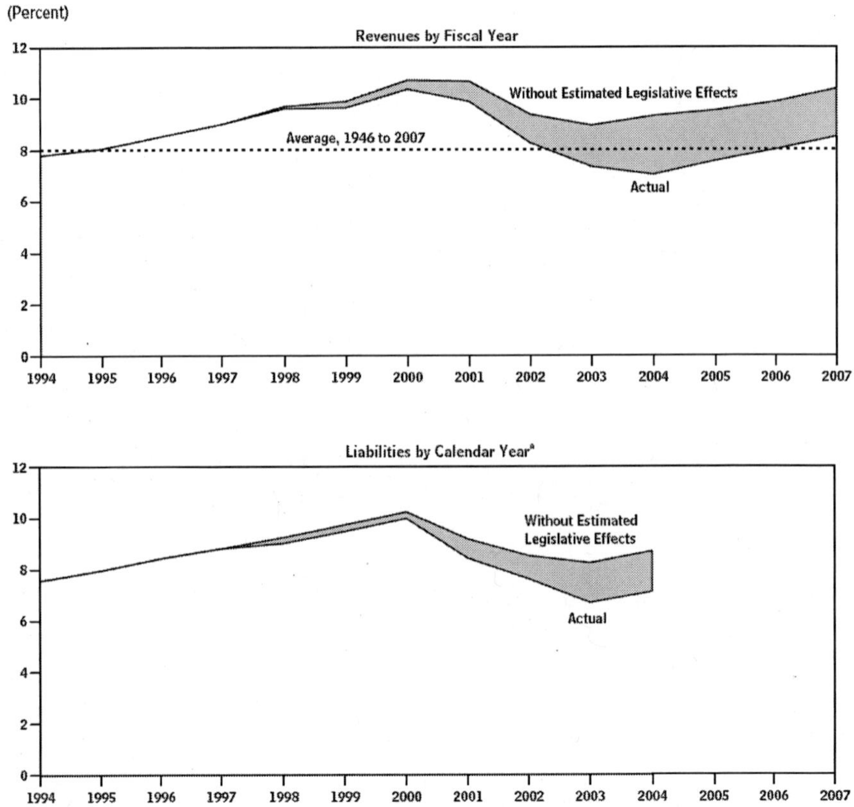

Source: Congressional Budget Office using data from the Joint Committee on Taxation for fiscal year revenues and data from the Internal Revenue Service's Statistics of Income for calendar year liabilities.

a. Data on liabilities are not available for years after 2004.

Figure 3. Individual Income Tax Revenues and Liabilities as a Share of Gross Domestic Product, Actual and Without Estimated Legislative Effects After 1994.

The estimated impact of legislation also does not include *any potential feedback effect of the tax changes on the economy.* Tax cuts can influence the overall level of demand in the economy in the short term and, on the supply side, can affect incentives to work and save over the longer term. The effect on liabilities of tax legislation enacted between 1994 and 2000 on liabilities was too small—relative to the overall economy—to have much effect on total economic output. The tax legislation enacted after 2000 probably had a modest effect. Most analysts agree that the approximately $36 billion paid out in rebates between July and December 2001 had some effect on the economy.[5] According to one estimate, the rebates boosted total consumption by 0.8 percent in the quarter the rebates were received and by 0.6 percent in the following quarters.[6] Those effects were probably short-lived, however. The reduced tax rates enacted in 2001 and 2003 increased incentives for people to work and save, but those supply-side effects generally take longer to have an impact on the economy. In addition, the tax legislation increased the budget deficit, and higher deficits tend to reduce economic growth over the medium and long term. Once all those factors are taken into account, the overall impact of the 2001 and 2003 tax legislation on the economy is likely to have been small through 2004.

CBO's analysis of the President's budgetary proposals for fiscal year 2006 suggests the potential order of magnitude of such feedback effects.[7] Although CBO analyzed the effects of the President's proposals taken as a whole, the major proposal in the budget was to extend provisions of EGTRRA and JGTRRA that are set to expire after 2010. The analysis found that, on average, the economic effect of the budgetary proposals could add up to 2 percent or offset up to 9 percent of the cost of the proposals over the medium term, depending on the assumptions used. Feedback effects in that range would have little impact on the estimates of the legislation-induced change in liabilities as a percentage of GDP. The estimated effect of EGTRRA and JGTRRA combined was to reduce income tax liabilities by 1.3 percent of GDP from 2000 to 2004. A positive feedback on liabilities at the upper end of the CBO analysis, for example, would lower that estimate by only 0.1 percentage point.

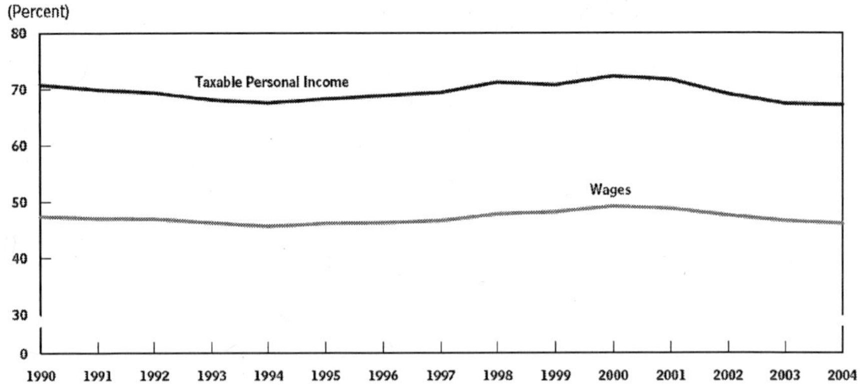

Source: Congressional Budget Office.

Figure 4. Taxable Personal Income and Wages as a Share of Gross Domestic Product, Calendar Years 1990 to 2004.

A Rising and Falling Individual Income Tax Base

A significant portion of the rise and fall of the income tax share of GDP stems from the rise and fall of the income tax base relative to total economic output. The tax base for individual income taxes is adjusted gross income, defined in the Internal Revenue Code as gross income from all sources minus certain deductions. To understand how AGI first grew more rapidly and then more slowly than the economy, it is useful to separate AGI into two components—income from current production, based on the income concepts that underlie the national income and product accounts (NIPAs), and income from other sources, particularly the realization of capital gains.

In the NIPAs, GDP measures aggregate economic activity on the product (or output) side, and gross domestic income (GDI) measures the same aggregate activity on the income side.[8] Personal income is the portion of GDI accruing to households. It comprises employees' compensation (including wages and salaries, employers' contributions to pensions and insurance, and employers' contributions for social insurance), proprietors' income, rental income, interest, dividends, and transfer payments from governments and businesses, less employees' and employers' contributions for social insurance, primarily Social Security and Medicare.

Taxable personal income (TPI) is the income measure based on the NIPAs that most closely corresponds to the portion of the individual income tax base that comes from current production. TPI includes the taxable components of personal income, plus employees' contributions for social insurance. It excludes tax-exempt forms of compensation such as employers' contributions for pensions, private health insurance, and other nontaxable fringe benefits.

Table 2. Contribution of Changes in the Individual Income Tax Base to Changes in Income Tax Liabilities as a Share of Gross Domestic Product, Calendar Years 1994 to 2004

Source of Change	1994–2000	2000–2004
	In Percentage Points	
TPI Growth More or Less Than GDP Growth	0.5	-0.6
AGI Growth More or Less Than TPI Growth[a]		
Capital gains growth	0.7	-0.6
Other AGI growth	0.2	0
Subtotal	0.9	-0.6
Total, individual income tax base	1.5	-1.2
As a Percentage of All Changes in Liabilities Relative to Gross Domestic Product		
TPI Growth More or Less Than GDP Growth	20	37
AGI Growth More or Less Than TPI Growtha		
Capital gains growth	28	42
Other AGI growth	7	0
Subtotal	35	42
Total, individual income tax base	55	79
Memorandum:		
All Changes (Percentage points)	2.7	-1.5

Source: Congressional Budget Office using data from the Internal Revenue Service's Statistics of Income.

Note: TPI = taxable personal income; GDP = gross domestic product; AGI = adjusted gross income.

a. Adjusted gross income has been modified to remove the impact of legislation since 1994.

TPI Growth More or Less than GDP Growth

Between 1994 and 2000, taxable personal income grew much faster than total economic output. The ratio of taxable personal income to GDP increased from 67.5 percent to 72.3 percent (see Figure 4). Wages are the largest component of TPI (68 percent in 2000), and their growth accounts for most of the excess growth in TPI relative to GDP over the 1994–2000 period. Personal dividend income and proprietors' income also grew faster than GDP but are much smaller components of TPI.

Over the 1994–2000 period, the accelerated growth in TPI raised the individual income tax share of GDP by 0.5 percentage points, or roughly 20 percent of the 2.7-percentage-point increase that would have occurred in the absence of legislation (see Table 2). That trend reversed, however, over the next four years. The TPI share of GDP fell from 72.3 percent in 2000 to 67.2 percent in 2004, eliminating the effects of growth in the earlier period. Wages grew more slowly than GDP over that period, accounting for much of the slower growth in TPI. The declining TPI share of GDP accounted for a drop of 0.6 percentage points in the individual income tax share of GDP between 2000 and 2004, or 37 percent of the 1.5-percentage-point decline that would have occurred in the absence of tax legislation.

AGI Growth More or Less than TPI Growth

Adjusted gross income—the tax base for individual income taxes— does not include all taxable personal income as measured in the national accounts. Certain items are specifically excluded by law. For example, employee contributions to 401(k) and 403(b) retirement accounts are included in TPI but not in AGI. Also, income earned by people who do not file tax returns is not included in AGI. If excluded income grew at a different rate from other income or if the growth in income of filers and nonfilers differed, it would show up as different growth rates of TPI and AGI.

AGI, however, does include a significant amount of income that is not included in TPI. Pension income is one example, and realized capital gains are another. Pension income and realized capital gains reported on tax returns do not reflect income from current production; rather, they reflect income that has been deferred from previous years and therefore are not included in TPI.

From 1994 to 2000, AGI grew faster than TPI, accounting for an increase of 0.9 percentage points in income tax liabilities as a share of GDP (see Table 2). That trend reversed from 2000 to 2004, with AGI growing more slowly than TPI, causing a drop of 0.6 percentage points in that share.

Changing amounts of capital gains realizations play an important role in explaining why AGI grew and then fell relative to GDP. From 1994 to 2000, realized capital gains grew much faster than GDP. The ratio of gains to GDP increased from 2.2 percent in 1994 to 6.6 percent by 2000 (see Figure 5). As a result of increased realizations, income tax liabilities from capital gains grew by $91 billion between 1994 and 2000, even with a reduction (from 28 percent to 20 percent) in the top tax rate on gains in 1997. The increase in capital gains liabilities accounted for almost 80 percent of the 0.9-percentagepoint increase in income tax liabilities as a percentage of GDP caused by AGI growth in excess of TPI and more than a quarter of the total increase in the tax share of GDP in the absence of legislation (see Table 2).

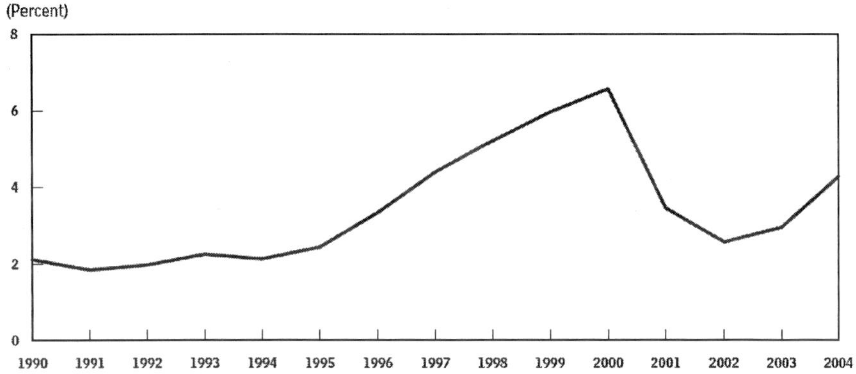

Source: Congressional Budget Office.

Figure 5. Realizations of Capital Gains as a Share of Gross Domestic Product, Calendar Years 1990 to 2004.

In contrast, between 2000 and 2004, GDP rose by 19.0 percent and AGI by 6.7 percent, partly because of a drop in capital gains realizations. The ratio of gains to GDP declined from 6.6 percent in 2000 to a low of 2.6 percent in 2002 and then rose to 4.3 percent in 2004. Tax liabilities from capital gains fell by $55 billion between 2000 and 2004. That decline was responsible for almost the entire drop of 0.6 percentage points in the income tax share of GDP caused by the difference between AGI growth and TPI growth during that period.

Those results were influenced by changes in the tax rates applicable to capital gains that were enacted in 1997 and 2003—but CBO has no clear basis for delineating how much of those outcomes was attributable to the enacted legislation. The Taxpayer Relief Act of 1997 reduced the top marginal tax rate on long-term gains from 28 percent to 20 percent. JGTRRA reduced the top rate on longterm gains from 20 percent to 15 percent starting in 2003; that reduction is scheduled to expire after 2010. Because taxpayers can choose when to realize capital gains (and losses), more gains are realized when tax rates are lower. However, over time, the increase in realizations induced by lower tax rates is not sufficient to offset the direct impact on revenues from the tax reduction itself, for two reasons. First, revenues will always increase by less than realizations following a tax cut because gains are taxed at the lower rate. For example, if the rate were lowered from 20 percent to 15 percent (a 25 percent reduction in the tax rate), realizations would need to increase by a third just to keep revenues unchanged. Second, increases in realizations are generally much larger in the short term than over the long term because some of the additional revenues in the short term come from gains that would have been realized in later years.

It is difficult to disentangle tax-induced changes in realizations from other factors that cause realizations to increase. Capital gains realizations rose by 45 percent in 1996 (before the 1997 tax cut) and by 40 percent in 1997 (after the tax cut). The increase was 25 percent in 1998. The increases in tax liabilities were larger in 1996—50 percent—but much smaller in the following two years, growing by 19 percent in 1997 and 12 percent in 1998.

Realizations also rose following the 2003 tax cut, by 20 percent in 2003 and by 54 percent in 2004. By contrast, tax liabilities increased by only 4 percent in 2003 and by 41 percent in 2004. Those increases came after a prolonged drop in both capital gains realizations and liabilities, however. Realizations in 2004 were still about 23 percent below their peak in 2000, and liabilities were about 43 percent below the 2000 level.

Separating the effects of changes in the tax rate from other factors affecting capital gains realizations is difficult. The best estimates of taxpayers' response to changes in the capital gains tax rate do not suggest a large revenue increase from additional realizations of capital gains— and certainly not an increase large enough to offset the losses from a lower rate.[9] Estimates of the effect of capital gains legislation on revenues include taxpayers' response to the changes in the tax rate on capital gains. Taking that effect into account, the Joint Committee on Taxation estimated at the time of enactment that the reduction in the capital gains rates in 1997 and 2003 would result in a small revenue loss through 2004.

Changes in the Effective Tax Rate on Adjusted Gross Income

Changes in income tax liabilities not accounted for by legislation or growth in adjusted gross income are explained by changes in the effective individual income tax rate—the ratio of income tax liabilities to AGI. A number of factors can cause the effective tax rate to rise or fall.

Per Capita TPI Growth More or Less than Inflation

Growth in real per capita income raises the effective tax rate. Because tax parameters, such as the tax brackets and the values of credits and deductions, are indexed to increases in consumer prices, only income growth in excess of price inflation will push more income into higher tax brackets. That phenomenon, known as real bracket creep, causes tax liabilities to grow as real per capita income grows over time; it is routinely incorporated into revenue projections whenever the economic projections forecast real income growth.

Changes in the Distribution of Income

Changes in the distribution of income also can increase the effective tax rate. Given the graduated structure of the individual income tax, increased concentration of income at the top of the distribution increases the effective tax rate because a large share of that taxable income is taxed at higher rates. Changes in the distribution of income can come from changes across and within sources of income. As a result of such changes, the income of higher-income taxpayers grew more rapidly than income for other taxpayers from 1994 to 2000, thereby raising the effective income tax rate (see Figure 6).

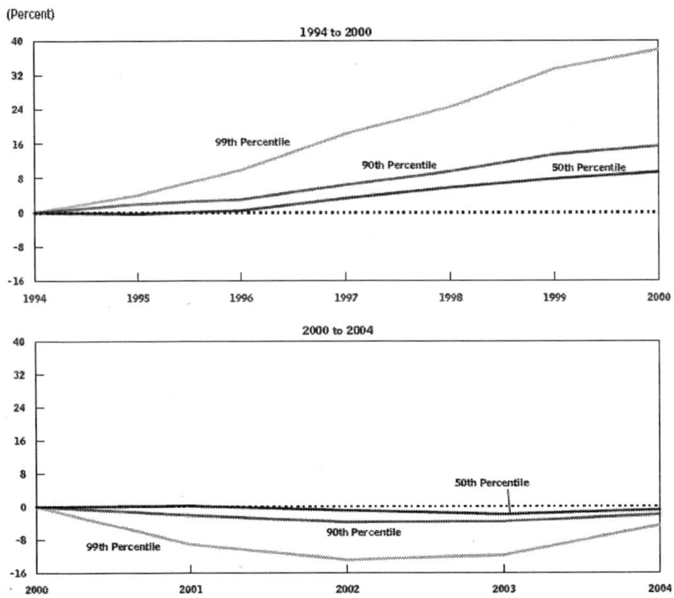

Source: Congressional Budget Office.

Figure 6. Percentage Growth in Adjusted Gross Income (Excluding Capital Gains) at the 50th, 90th, and 99th Income Percentiles, Calendar Years 1994 to 2004.

Changes Across Sources of Income

Changes across sources of income will increase effective tax rates if high-income filers receive a disproportionate share of the source of income with the fastest growth. For example, a rapid rise in partnership income, which accrues predominantly to upper-income taxpayers, would raise the effective rate. Conversely, relatively more growth in sources of income accruing primarily to low-income filers would decrease the average effective tax rate because more income would be taxed at lower rates.

Certain forms of income that tend to flow to higher-income individuals grew more rapidly than other types of income between 1994 and 2000 but more slowly between 2000 and 2004 (see Figure 6). For example, income from S corporations rose from 1.9 percent of adjusted gross income (excluding capital gains) in 1994 to 2.2 percent by 2000.[10] In contrast, wages as a share of AGI (excluding capital gains) fell from 81 percent to 78 percent during the same period. Because the tax rate on S corporation income is, on average, twice the rate on wages, the shift in composition between the two sources of income raised the average tax rate on AGI.[11] Other highly taxed sources also grew more quickly during this period, raising the effective tax rate on AGI.

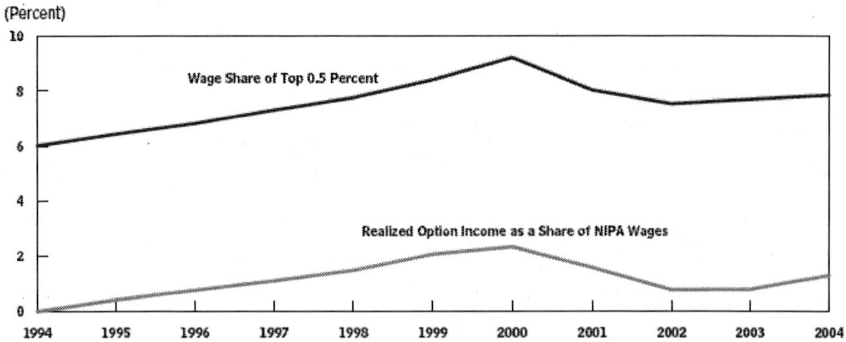

Source: Congressional Budget Office using data from Scott Jaquette, Matthew Knittel, and Karl Russo, Recent Trends in Stock Options, OTA Working Paper 89 (Washington, D.C.: Department of the Treasury, Office of Tax Analysis, March 2003).

Notes: Nonqualified stock options can be granted in unlimited amounts and, for purposes of the individual income tax, are treated the same as wages once they are exercised and the stock is purchased.

NIPA = national income and product accounts.

Figure 7. Share of Wages Accruing to the Top 0.5 Percent of Earners and Income from Nonqualified Stock Options as a Share of Wages, Calendar Years 1994 to 2004.

Changes within Sources of Income

In addition to differential growth in sources of income taxed at higher rates, changes to the distribution of income within sources can increase the effective tax rate. For example, the share of wages going to the top one-half of one percent of wage earners rose sharply, from 6 percent of all wages in 1994 to just over 9 percent in 2000 (see Figure 7). One reason for the rapid growth was the rise in income gained from exercising nonqualified stock options over this period.[12] Nonqualified stock options can be granted in unlimited amounts and, for purposes of the individual income tax, are treated the same as wages once they are exercised and the stock is purchased. Although not all option income was claimed by taxpayers at the top end of the wage distribution, much of it was realized by highly compensated taxpayers, one of the likely causes of the rise in the wage share of GDP over this period.[13] The increase in option income along with the previous evidence on the rapid rise of capital gains realizations suggests that the stock market has played an important role in the rise and fall of individual income tax liabilities since 1994.[14]

Box 1. Effect of the Alternative Minimum Tax on Individual Income Tax Receipts

Although the alternative minimum tax (AMT), if left unchanged, will have a significant effect on federal income tax revenues in the near future, the AMT played only a small role in explaining the rise and fall of individual income tax revenues between 1994 and 2004. The AMT accounted for just $2 billion of income tax revenues in 1994, $9 billion in 2000, and $13 billion in 2004. AMT liabilities were less than 1.0 percent of total individual income tax liabilities before 2003, rising to 1.3 percent in 2003 and 1.6 percent in 2004.

The AMT is a parallel tax system originally designed to ensure that high-income taxpayers who faced little liability under the regular tax system would pay some amount of income tax. The tax base for the AMT includes several items that are excluded from taxation under the regular income tax. For example, taxpayers cannot claim personal exemptions or the standard deduction under the AMT, and if they itemize they cannot claim a deduction for state and local taxes. In lieu of personal exemptions and the standard deduction, the AMT allows a sizable exemption—$35,750 for a single tax filer and $45,000 for a married couple (temporarily increased to $44,350 and $66,250 in 2007).

The exemptions are phased out for highincome filers. Income in excess of the exemption is subject to a tax rate of 26 percent initially and 28 percent after income exceeds a certain threshold ($175,000 in 2007). Most tax filers face no AMT liability at present, but that will change in time because—unlike the regular income tax—the exemption amounts for the AMT are not adjusted for inflation.

Recent tax legislation provided temporary relief starting in 2001 by increasing the AMT exemption, but the most recent increases in the exemption expired at the end of 2007. If there are no changes in current law, by 2010 the AMT will account for $90 billion of individual income tax revenues.[1] That amount will decline in 2011 because the expiration of the Economic Growth and Tax Relief Reconciliation Act of 2001 will increase regular income tax liabilities and thus decrease the amount of taxes collected under the AMT. In years after 2011, AMT liability will increase as incomes rise relative to the fixed AMT exemptions.

[1] See Congressional Budget Office, *The Alternative Minimum Tax* (April 15, 2004), for a more thorough explanation of the AMT and its impact on income tax revenues.

Other Factors

Other, minor factors also contributed to the change in the effective tax rate from 1994 to 2004.has played an important role in the rise and fall of individual income tax liabilities since 1994.[14]

Other Factors

Other, minor factors also contributed to the change in the effective tax rate from 1994 to 2004. Changes in the ratio of itemized deductions to AGI can change the effective tax rate. In general, itemized deductions grow with income. Some itemized deductions, such as those for state and local taxes, are directly linked to income, although the deduction is based on actual tax payments, which may occur in the tax year that follows the year in which the income is reported. Other deductions may have only an indirect connection to income. For example, mortgage interest deductions are linked to past and current mortgage interest rates. However, as income rises, households may take on more mortgage debt, creating a longer-run link between income and interest deductions. Even if deductions were linked to income, those links would probably take place with a lag, which would tend to cause effective tax rates to rise when income is rising and to fall when income is declining. Itemized deductions grew relative to AGI throughout the entire period, slightly offsetting some of the increase in effective tax rates from 1994 to 2000 and slightly adding to the decrease from 2000 to 2004.

Exercising incentive stock options can generate additional tax liability under the alternative minimum tax (AMT) without generating additional AGI under the regular income tax, thereby raising the effective tax rate on AGI.[15] A noticeable increase in this activity contributed to a bump in taxes collected from the AMT in 2000 to a level that was $3 billion above 1999 liabilities.[16] However, the AMT does not play a large role in explaining changes in individual income tax liabilities from 1994 to 2004 (see Box 1). Changing demographics can also raise or lower the effective tax rate through changes in taxpayers' filing status and the number of exemptions claimed, as can growth in the number of taxpayers claiming tax credits and the amount of credits claimed. Those factors, however, probably had only a small effect.

Table 3. Contribution of Changes in the Effective Tax Rate on Adjusted Gross Income to Changes in Income Tax Liabilities as a Share of Gross Domestic Product, Calendar Years 1994 to 2004

Source of Change	1994–2000	2000–2004
	In Percentage Points	
Per Capita TPI Growth More or Less Than Inflation	0.8	-0.3
Income Distribution and Other Factors	0.4	-0.1
Total, effective tax rate on AGI	1.2	-0.3
	As a Percentage of All Changes in Liabilities Relative to Gross Domestic Product	
Per Capita TPI Growth More or Less Than Inflation	28	17
Income Distribution and Other Factors	16	4
Total, effective tax rate on AGI	45	21
Memorandum:		
All Changes (Percentage points)	2.7	-1.5

Source: Congressional Budget Office using data from the Internal Revenue Service's Statistics of Income.

Notes: Estimates exclude capital gains.

TPI = taxable personal income; AGI = adjusted gross income.

Impact of Changes in the Effective Tax Rate

From 1994 to 2000, the increase in the effective tax rate accounted for 1.2 percentage points of the 2.7-percentage-point increase in the ratio of liabilities to GDP that would have occurred in the absence of legislation—or about 45 percent of the total increase (see Table 3). Conversely, from 2000 to 2004 income at the upper end fell by more than income at other points in the distribution, contributing to a decline in the effective income tax rate. Over that period, that lower rate accounted for a drop of 0.3 percentage points in the ratio of liabilities to GDP—about 21 percent of the decline that would have occurred without legislation.

Separating the effect of growth in real per capita income from the effects of changes in the distribution of income is difficult. Real per capita AGI (excluding capital gains) grew by 24 percent between 1994 and 2000. The estimated elasticity of income tax liabilities with respect to real income growth is roughly 1.5—that is, growth of 10 percent in real per capita AGI results in growth of 10 percent in real per capita AGI results in growth of 15 percent in income tax liabilities.[17] With that elasticity, the 24 percent growth in AGI (excluding capital gains) would have increased the ratio of liabilities to GDP by 0.8 percentage points as a result of real bracket creep, out of the 1.2-percentage-point increase resulting from changes in the effective tax rate. Between 2000 and 2004, real per capita AGI (excluding capital gains) declined by 4 percent, which would have lowered the ratio of liabilities to GDP by 0.3 percentage points. Thus, over that period, real bracket creep accounted for most of the change attributable to variations in the effective tax rate.

CHANGES IN INCOME TAX REVENUES SINCE 2004

The detailed calendar year data on individual income liabilities needed to identify the source of the increase in individual income taxes between 2004 and 2007 are not yet fully available. One can, however, identify some of the factors responsible for that increase from information related to fiscal year tax revenues.

Between fiscal years 2004 and 2007, individual income tax revenues grew from 7.0 percent to 8.5 percent of GDP—about 1.5 percentage points of GDP. In both years, revenues were lower than they would have been without the enactment of various pieces of legislation since 1994, but the reduction was larger in 2004 than in 2007, mostly because of timing effects. Thus, although the ratio of income tax revenues to GDP was lower in both years than it would have been in the absence of the 2001 and 2003 tax cuts, the ratio rose between 2004 and 2007 because of the smaller impact in the later year. Excluding any potential macroeconomic effects, the legislation enacted since 1994 (including EGTRRA and JGTRRA) accounted for an estimated 0.5 percentage points of that change.[18]

The remaining 1 percentage point of the increase in individual income tax revenues was the combined result of some factors that acted to reduce revenues relative to GDP and others that acted to raise them. Taxable personal income—principally wages and salaries—rose relative to GDP, increasing receipts relative to GDP by about 0.1 percentage point. Higher realizations of capital gains (including any effects associated with legislated reductions in tax rates) added about 0.4 percentage points. The remaining 0.6 percentage points of the increase in individual income tax revenues relative to GDP resulted from real bracket creep and a variety of potential factors that cannot be evaluated fully until more complete data are available. Such potential factors include shifts in the share of aggregate taxable income accruing to households with higher marginal tax rates; changes in taxable income relative to the measures of personal income in the NIPAs; and changes in retirement income, the alternative minimum tax, and tax deductions.

End Notes

[1] CBO did not adjust the estimates to remove the effects of legislation on revenues from capital gains. Although legislation was responsible for some change in revenues from capital gains over this period, those effects are treated together with other changes in capital gains revenues because it is difficult to separate the impact of legislation from other factors that caused revenues from capital gains to rise and fall.

[2] Receipts from income taxes paid by estates and trusts, or fiduciary income taxes, followed a pattern similar to that for individual income taxes, though the percentage change was much greater. In fiscal year 1995, fiduciary tax collections were estimated to be $5 billion. In fiscal year 2000, they grew to about $18 billion, but by fiscal year 2003 they were down to about $8 billion.

[3] CBO's estimates are based on the Joint Committee on Taxation's estimates at the time of enactment, modified to account for changes in the economic forecast and actual receipts.

[4] The somewhat larger difference for 2004 reflects the effect of legislation enacted in 2003 on the timing of tax revenues.

[5] See Congressional Budget Office, Options for Responding to Short-Term Economic Weakness (January 2008).

[6] David Johnson, Jonathan Parker, and Nicholas S. Souleles, "Household Expenditure and the Income Tax Rebates of 2001," *American Economic Review*, vol. 96, no. 5 (December 2006), pp. 1589–1610.

[7] Congressional Budget Office, *An Analysis of the President's Budgetary Proposals for Fiscal Year 2006* (March 2005), Chapter 2. The estimates are for the impact of all of the President's proposals from 2011 to 2016, including proposed changes in revenues and outlays. Proposals other than the extension of the expiring tax cuts had relatively minor net economic effects. More recent editions of that annual report encompass proposals other than the extension of the expiring tax cuts. Those other proposals would have additional economic effects, which is why those studies were not used in this analysis.

[8] Total production and total income should be equal; however, a statistical discrepancy exists between the two and is reported in the NIPAs. In 1994, that discrepancy was $143 billion, meaning that measured national product was $143 billion greater than measured national income. The discrepancy fell after 1994 and eventually became negative, indicating that measured national income was higher than national product. By 2000, the discrepancy had reached -$127 billion. The trend reversed course, and by 2004 the discrepancy was $19 billion. Although it is not possible to assign the statistical discrepancy to either the product side or the income side of the national accounts, the discrepancy could account for some of the differences in the growth of GDP and in the income tax base over the 1994–2004 period.

[9] See Leonard E. Burman, *The Labyrinth of Capital Gains Tax Policy* (Washington, D.C.: Brookings Institution Press, 1999), Chapter 4; Jane G. Gravelle, *The Economic Effects of Taxing Capital Income* (Cambridge, Mass.: MIT Press, 1994), Chapter 6; and George Zodrow, "Economic Analysis of Capital Gains Taxation: Realizations, Revenues, Efficiency, and Equity," *Tax Law Review*, vol. 48, no. 3 (1990), pp. 419–527.

[10] Gains are excluded from the calculation because they are taxed under a separate rate schedule.

[11] These calculations of average tax rates were done on the 1994 Statistics of Income file. The amount of taxable income in each tax bracket was allocated to each component of income in proportion to that component's share of total income (excluding capital gains).

[12] See Scott Jaquette, Matthew Knittel, and Karl Russo, *Recent Trends in Stock Options*, OTA Working Paper 89 (Department of the Treasury, Office of Tax Analysis, March 2003).

[13] Although option income may explain some of the rise in individual income taxes because of the impact on the distribution of wages, the income itself may have had a minimal impact on overall receipts. The income claimed by individuals was simultaneously a deduction for corporations under the corporate income tax.

[14] The stock market also affects receipts in other ways. Receipts based on asset levels, such as taxable retirement distributions and estate and gift tax receipts, were also affected by the rise and fall in the stock market since 1994. Because asset levels grow differently than GDP, receipts associated with those assets will move differently as well. For more information on the impact of the stock market, see Congressional Budget Office, *Revenue Projections and the Stock Market* (December 20, 2002).

[15] Unlike nonqualified stock options, incentive stock options can be offered only in limited amounts and are normally subject to the individual income tax when the stock is sold, not when the options are exercised. However, exercising such options can generate liability under the AMT.

[16] See Shelly K. Schwartz, "Beware Stock Option Taxes" (April 10, 2001), money.cnn.com/2001/04/10/living/q_stockoptions/ index.htm.

[17] The 1.5 elasticity is with respect to tax liabilities excluding capital gains, and the calculations were done on tax return incomes exclusive of capital gains. (Since most gains are taxed at the top rate, little real bracket creep is associated with them.) The calculation was done using the consumer price index, which is relevant for constructing the tax brackets in each

year. It assumes that incomes grow evenly across the income distribution and is meant to illustrate how much to expect from real income growth. The actual change in income was not evenly distributed because of differential growth in various sources of income and because of changes in the distribution within sources.

[18] These estimates of revenues exclude the impact of legislation on capital gains, as did the estimates of liabilities over the 1994–2004 period.

In: Tax Distribution and Revenue Analyses... ISBN: 978-1-61324-421-0
Editor: Anthony N. Treviso © 2011 Nova Science Publishers, Inc.

Chapter 4

IMPROVING CBO'S METHODOLOGY FOR PROJECTING INDIVIDUAL INCOME TAX REVENUES*

The Congress of the United States, Congressional Budget Office

PREFACE

In preparing its annual report on the budget outlook, and updates to that report during the course of the year, the Congressional Budget Office (CBO) projects revenues from the federal individual income tax. This background paper discusses two possible ways to use information about tax collections to improve CBO's projections of tax receipts: Explicitly using the information provided by recent tax collections to adjust the projections, and basing the projections on multiple years of information from tax returns rather than relying on just the most recently available year. The results of CBO's analysis suggest that combining the two approaches—that is, using the information from recent tax collections and relying on multiple years of tax return information—can modestly improve the near-term projection of individual income tax revenues. Those findings have led CBO to use that combination of approaches in estimating revenues in recent years.

* This is an edited, reformatted and augmented version of a The Congress of the United States, Congressional Budget Office's publication Pub. No. 4038, dated February 2011.

Kurt Seibert, Mark Booth, and David Weiner of CBO's Tax Analysis Division wrote the paper with assistance from Regis Barnichon, formerly of CBO, under the guidance of Frank Sammartino. Robert Arnold and Janet Holtzblatt of CBO and George Plesko of the University of Connecticut's School of Business provided helpful comments. (The assistance of an external reviewer implies no responsibility for the final product, which rests solely with CBO.)

Leah Mazade edited the paper, Chris Howlett proofread it, and Jeanine Rees prepared the report for publication. Monte Ruffin produced the print copies, Linda Schimmel coordinated the print distribution, and Simone Thomas prepared the electronic version for CBO's Web site (www.cbo.gov).

Douglas W. Elmendorf
Director
February 2011

SUMMARY AND INTRODUCTION

Each January in *The Budget and Economic Outlook*, the Congressional Budget Office (CBO) publishes its projections of federal revenues spanning 11 years: the current fiscal year (that is, the fiscal year already under way at that point), the "budget year" (that is, the first full year after the year in which the projections are produced), and the nine fiscal years that follow. Those projections incorporate the assumption that the laws affecting revenues remain unchanged.[1] Since 1997, receipts of individual income taxes have differed from CBO's January projections for the current year by an average of about 6 percent—or by an average of 0.4 percent of gross domestic product (GDP). On average, receipts of individual income taxes for the budget year have differed from the projections made in January of the previous year by about 11 percent (1.0 percent of GDP). All of those differences have been calculated so that they exclude the effects of legislation enacted after the projections were prepared. They have also been calculated without regard to whether the discrepancies were positive or negative—that is, whether CBO overestimated or underestimated actual receipts— and are known as mean absolute errors.[2]

An analysis of the errors in CBO's past projections of individual income tax revenues suggests that, over time, the agency's estimates are about as likely to be too high as too low. For the years since 1997, positive and negative errors have largely offset each other; so, for example, the average *net* error over that time in CBO's projections for the current fiscal year is 0.6

percent, and the average *net* error for the budget year is 1.3 percent (less than 0.1 percent of GDP in both cases).[3] Nevertheless, CBO's analysis also suggests that errors in the projections of revenues for the current and budget years tend to be correlated over time; that is, if the projections made in one January for the current year and the budget year were too low, the projections made the next January would probably also be lower than actual revenues in those years.

This paper analyzes two approaches for improving the results from the model that CBO uses to project revenues from individual income taxes.[4] The results of this analysis have been incorporated in CBO's revenue forecasting.

In the first approach, CBO sought to determine the best way to use the most recent information about tax collections to minimize errors in its forecasts. When actual collections differ from projections, forecasters must judge whether the discrepancy they observe is a temporary deviation or the beginning of a longer-term trend and thus whether and by how much to adjust the model's projections of future revenues to reflect that discrepancy. Such determinations are complicated, though, because detailed tax return data that could identify the sources of the difference are not available for some time. In the absence of such data, CBO examined whether the accuracy of its projections would improve if it simply assumed that actual revenues would differ from the model's projection in future years by the same percentage that they differed in the most recent year for which actual revenues were known.

In the second approach, CBO analyzed the improvement to be gained from using additional years of tax return data as the basis for its projections. CBO's individual income tax model starts with the most recent year of detailed tax return data available. But those so-called base-year data may not be representative of longer-term trends. Therefore, CBO investigated whether the model might achieve more-accurate results by producing multiple projections using tax return data from different years (rather than data from only a single year) as the starting point and averaging the projections.

Using a simplified version of its individual income tax model and examining projections for the 1984–2005 period, CBO evaluated various versions of those two approaches as well as combinations of the two. CBO's findings included the following:

- Projections of tax liabilities (what taxpayers owe) were more accurate—but only in the very short term—when CBO adjusted the model's results by the percentage error in those results in the most recent year for which actual revenues were known (called the "alignment year" in this paper).

- The use of multiple years of detailed tax return data reduced the size of the error in CBO's projections compared with the use of only the most recent year of such data. Using four years of tax return data to produce four separate projections, and then averaging them, yielded the best overall results.
- A combination of the two approaches was better than either one by itself. Of the options that CBO examined, the combination that was most effective in reducing errors was to average projections based on the four most recent years of tax return data and to adjust the estimated liabilities for the first year by 50 percent of the alignment-year error.

Those improvements have limitations, however. The reduction in the size of the errors is small relative to the errors seen before making those adjustments. The reason is that the use of the most recent information can do little to reduce the uncertainty that surrounds the future course of the economy and the rate of growth of income in the tax base. Also, the degree of improvement in the projections' accuracy declines rapidly over the 10-year forecast horizon.

Analyzing CBO's Estimates of Individual Income Tax Revenues

Studies that have examined CBO's historical "track record" in forecasting revenues have concluded that although errors in its projections are equally likely to be too high as too low, revisions to the projections and the projections' deviations from actual outcomes have been correlated over time.[5] For example, one study (by Alan J. Auerbach) examined 10-year revenue forecasts produced from 1986 to 1999 and found that when CBO increased (or lowered) its revenue projections from one forecast to the next, it tended to raise (or lower) them again in the next forecast. Another study (by Rudolph G. Penner) looked at CBO's projections over the 1984–2005 period and found that underestimates (or overestimates) of revenues for a year tended to be followed by underestimates (or overestimates) of revenues in the following year's forecast.

Both findings suggest that CBO was not incorporating new information quickly enough into its forecasting methodology.

An analysis of CBO's forecasting record could indicate some ways to improve the accuracy of the agency's projections, but several factors complicate such an assessment.

- Forecasting methods change over time; the models and methods in use today would have produced different results than the results produced years ago with different methods. For example, adjustments to CBO's individual income tax model to reflect the most recent information from tax collections have changed over the years, making it difficult to isolate the effects of different methods of incorporating that information.
- Past errors in forecasting may have occurred for reasons unrelated to the two issues that are the focus of this analysis. For instance, CBO may have projected tax liabilities correctly but misestimated the fiscal year in which payments were made.
- The number of forecasts that CBO has produced over the years is relatively small for the purposes of statistical analysis and the development of reliable conclusions.
- Numerous changes in the tax code make it difficult to separate the effects of those changes from the effects of other factors. Because CBO's forecasts by design incorporate the assumption that for the 10-year projection period, current tax laws remain unaltered by future legislation, any assessment of CBO's track record in revenue forecasting must take into account the effects of subsequent legislation.

Those complicating factors would affect any analysis that relied on identifying and assessing errors in CBO's historical forecasting record. As a result, for this analysis, CBO instead recreated past forecasts by using a simplified version of its individual income tax model. This paper addresses the relationship between the error in CBO's estimate for the last known liability year and the errors in future years in CBO's model for projecting individual income tax liabilities.[6] It does not address other elements and characteristics of errors in the estimates of individual income tax revenues, nor does it address errors in projections of revenues from other sources.

THE TIMING OF TAX PAYMENTS AND THE AVAILABILITY OF TAX DATA

Two factors are critical in understanding the relationship between CBO's individual income tax model and its projections of tax receipts: the timing of those tax collections and the lag in the availability of detailed data from tax returns.

CBO's individual income tax model produces estimates of tax liabilities for a particular tax year—generally, a calendar year. Those projections of liabilities are then converted into projections of collections by incorporating expectations about when taxpayers will pay what they owe. Some portion of those liabilities will be collected throughout the calendar year in the form of withheld and estimated tax payments; most of the rest will be collected the next year, after tax returns are filed.

In January 2010, for example, CBO released projections of federal revenues from the individual income tax for fiscal years 2010 through 2020. Those projections were based on estimates of liabilities generated by CBO's individual income tax model for 2009 through 2020. The projection of receipts for fiscal year 2010 (the "current year," according to the terminology in this paper) reflected payments for liabilities that the model projected for both calendar year 2009 and calendar year 2010 (see the bottom of Figure 1). The projection for the next year, fiscal year 2011 (the "budget year," in this paper's lexicon), reflected payments for liabilities that the model projected for calendar years 2010 and 2011.

The tax return data used in CBO's individual income tax model lag several years behind the year in which the projections are made, for multiple reasons. Although most people file their returns for one year by April of the next year, many taxpayers receive an extension for filing until October. It then takes the Internal Revenue Service (IRS) several months to compile the information; typically, details from the tax returns, in the form of a sample of returns that the IRS publishes as the Statistics of Income (SOI) Individual Income Tax File for that tax year, are available the following summer. CBO must then analyze and incorporate those data into its forecasting model.

For example, for the projections released in January 2010, the base year of data for CBO's tax model was 2007, the latest year for which detailed tax return data were available. (Tax returns for that year were filed in 2008, and the detailed data became available in 2009.) CBO used those data to estimate what the tax returns in the 2007 SOI file (roughly 335,000 records) would look like for liability years 2008 through 2020 by adjusting the returns on the basis of actual and projected growth in the population and in income. Although tax returns for 2008 were not yet available at the time of the January 2010 forecast, CBO had an estimate of tax liabilities for 2008 (based on actual tax collections in fiscal years 2008 and 2009) that it could use to adjust the results from the model and improve its projections for subsequent years.

FORECASTING TAX RECEIPTS

CBO's individual income tax model relies on a microsimulation approach, using a sample of tax returns that reflects the diversity of households in the U.S. economy. The model is designed to capture certain characteristics of the population (for example, the distribution of tax filers by age) and how those characteristics interact with provisions of the tax code.[7] Different tax provisions apply to different types of income and families. Because both the tax code and the characteristics of the population are changing over time, the microsimulation approach allows the model to reflect interactions between changes in the law and in the filing population's characteristics that affect revenues.

Once the sample of tax returns for a particular year has become available, CBO "ages" the sample from the base year to subsequent years by using actual data on the growth of the population and of income for the initial years and its projections of such growth for later years. CBO estimates changes in the different types of income reported on tax returns (such as earnings, interest, and dividends) on the basis of two factors: the actual history of comparable measures of those types of income available in the national income and product accounts (NIPAs) and CBO's projections of those measures for future years.[8] The NIPA measures of income do not exactly match the corresponding tax return measures because of differences in what each covers. In addition, certain kinds of income reported on tax returns, such as capital gains realizations and retirement income, have no analog in the NIPAs, and CBO must estimate those components of income separately. CBO also incorporates population growth into the model, using detailed estimates developed by the Social Security Administration, which are disaggregated by age, sex, and marital status.

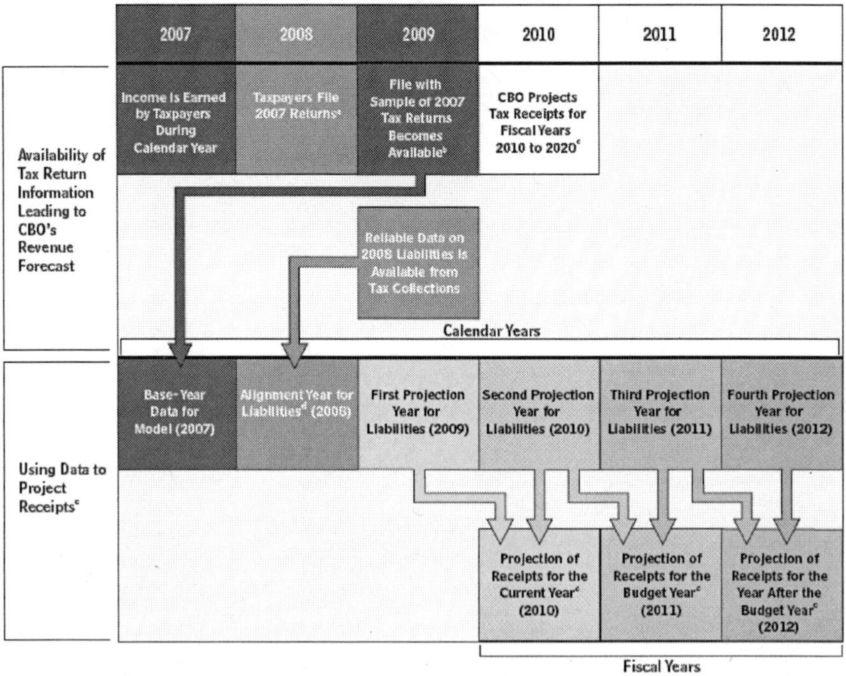

Source: Congressional Budget Office.

Note: CBO's January 2010 revenue forecast included projections of receipts and liabilities through 2020. (The years 2013 to 2020 are not shown above.)

[a] The initial deadline for filing taxes for a year is April 15 of the subsequent year, but taxpayers can automatically receive a six-month filing extension.

[b] That is, the Internal Revenue Service's Statistics of Income Individual Income Tax File.

[c] Receipts are based on liabilities from the current year and the previous year because some payments in the current year are for liabilities incurred in the previous year.

[d] The alignment year is a year for which total tax receipts are known but detailed tax statistics are not yet available. The actual results for that year can be used to create an adjustment for the rest of the projection horizon by comparing the results from CBO's model for that year with actual individual income tax liabilities and then adjusting the model's projections for the remaining years of the horizon by that first-year difference.

Figure 1. Timeline for Information Used in CBO's Revenue Projections Released in January 2010.

CBO calculates the tax liability of each taxpayer in the sample by applying those estimates of changes in the distribution of income and the population as well as the effects of scheduled changes in the tax code. To generate total individual income tax liability for the entire population, CBO applies the weights from the sample—that is, the adjustments made to reflect the number of returns that each individual return in the sample represents. CBO then converts the estimate of total individual income tax liability from the model into projections of tax receipts, which measure how and when those liabilities will be collected in each fiscal year—specifically, how much will be collected through withholding, estimated payments, and the final payments taxpayers make when they file their returns.

The last step in forecasting receipts is to use the latest information on tax collections, which is available a year before the IRS's detailed tax return sample is released, to adjust the results of the model's projections of liabilities. For example, for CBO's January 2010 revenue forecast, the latest detailed tax return data covered the 2007 tax liability year. However, CBO used information about tax collections to estimate liabilities for the 2008 liability year, calculating overall taxes owed by adding together all of the tax payments made for that year: those for taxes withheld during calendar year 2008; the estimated tax payments made in 2008 (in April, June, and September) and in January 2009; and the final payments made and refunds issued for returns filed in 2009.[9] Once CBO had developed that estimate, it compared the projection of liabilities for 2008 from the model with its estimate of liabilities based on payments to determine whether and how to adjust the model's projections for other years of the forecast horizon.[10]

Why the Results of CBO's Model Differ from Actual Outcomes

When fuller information from tax returns becomes available, the discrepancies between actual tax receipts and CBO's projections can be traced, in part, to misestimates of the inputs for CBO's projection model. (For example, the actual rate of growth of incomes might have been different from what CBO projected.)[11] Other potential sources of errors include factors that affect liabilities but that the individual income tax model does not properly reflect. In particular:

- The most recent NIPA historical measures of wages and other types of income may contain inaccuracies that will be revised later, when better data become available.

- The relationship between categories of income in the NIPAs and the corresponding categories on tax returns may have changed. For example, wages recorded on tax returns may not grow at the same rate as do wages measured in the NIPAs.
- The income distribution may have changed in unexpected ways, causing misestimates of the average tax rates that taxpayers face.[12]
- The effects of recent legislative changes may be reflected incorrectly.
- Other assumptions used in CBO's model—for example, about deductions, credits, and other components that are critical for determining tax liabilities but that are not part of CBO's macroeconomic projections—may be incorrect.

In certain cases, the divergence of CBO's revenue projections from actual outcomes might reflect some temporary factor. For example, income from the exercising of stock options was substantially higher in 1999 and 2000 than in previous years. That activity boosted total income and the share of income attributable to high-income filers—but only for those two years (the increase did not continue in the future). In other cases, an effect might persist. For instance, if CBO's estimate of the "cost" of a new tax credit was too low for the first year—because more people claimed the credit than CBO had expected—more people would probably claim it in future years than CBO had initially projected.

Until specific information on the sources of a divergence becomes available from tax returns, CBO has only limited data from which to determine whether the likely causes of a misestimate will prevail throughout the forecast period and whether the agency should adjust its projections accordingly. In those circumstances, CBO could follow one of two approaches:

- Assume that the misestimate resulted entirely from temporary phenomena and make no adjustments to the model's projections for the forecast period, or
- Assume that some or all of the discrepancy will continue into the forecast period and carry forward as an adjustment all or a portion of the amount by which the projection was too high or too low.

CBO generally follows that second approach, which is examined in the remainder of this paper, along with other methods for reflecting historical tax data in the agency's projections.

MEASURING FORECASTING ERRORS USING CBO'S SIMPLIFIED TAX MODEL

In analyzing the effectiveness of changes in its projection methods, CBO used a simplified tax model (STM) to more easily examine patterns of errors among different forecasts. The STM generates forecasts similar to those from the microsimulation model that CBO uses for its official forecasts. The differences between the forecasts generated by the STM and actual liabilities, expressed as a percentage of actual liabilities, were used to measure the errors in CBO's revenue forecasting. (For more information about CBO's simplified tax model, see Appendix A.)

For this analysis, CBO used the STM to project individual income tax liabilities for as many as eight years beyond each of the base years 1984 through 2005 (for which detailed tax return data are available). CBO then compared those projections with actual liabilities to measure differences between the two for various projection years. As an example, in 1984, individual income tax liabilities totaled $309 billion. Starting with that amount, CBO used the most recent of its macroeconomic forecasts that would have been available—that is, the one issued in January 1987—and combined that forecast with information on income, tax rates, and tax rate elasticities derived from the tax return data to estimate total liabilities for future years.[13]

For example, CBO projected tax liabilities for 1985, 1988, and 1992 (for the purposes of this paper, "base year + 1," "base year + 4," and "base year + 8") of $334 billion, $444 billion, and $492 billion, respectively (see Figure 2). The projections diverged from the actual results for those years, overestimating liabilities by $3 billion for 1985, underestimating them by $27 billion for 1988, and overestimating them by $69 billion for 1992. Because the absolute size of such differences would tend to grow as the value of income tax liabilities grew, using that measure would make it difficult to compare the discrepancies over time. As a result, CBO "normalized" the errors by measuring them as a percentage of actual liabilities. For the previous example, actual liabilities differed from CBO's projections for 1985, 1988, and 1992 by -1.0 percent, 6.1 percent, and -13.9 percent, respectively (see Table 1).

Because actual data on income tax liabilities are available for the year after the base year, CBO can make certain adjustments to its estimates in that year. Thus, the year after the base year (base year + 1) is termed the "alignment year" in this analysis, the second year after the base year (base year

+ 2) is termed the first projection year, the third year after the base year is termed the second projection year, and so forth.

The years referenced here are liability years in the model, not the fiscal years of CBO's revenue projections. In the previous example, the first fiscal year covered in the January 1987 projections was what was then the current fiscal year—1987; the official revenue projection for that year was based on the (in this case, microsimulation) model's estimates of liabilities for 1986 and 1987. The projection for fiscal year 1988, the budget year, was based on the model's results for 1987 and 1988.

ESTIMATING THE POTENTIAL IMPROVEMENT IN THE ACCURACY OF CBO'S REVENUE FORECASTING

The accuracy of a forecast is the degree to which its projected values are narrowly dispersed around the actual outcomes. The root mean square error (RMSE) is a metric that can be used with different forecasting methodologies to compare their effects and to suggest the best method—at least over time—of using information from the error in the projection for the first year of a forecast period to improve the forecast's accuracy in subsequent years. The RMSE is calculated by first squaring each of the errors in the projections for a forecast period and then taking the square root of the arithmetic average of the squared errors. (For example, if the errors in three projections were 2 percent, -3 percent, and 4 percent, the RMSE would equal 3.1 percent, the square root of the average of the three squared errors [(4 + 9 + 16)/3 = 9.7)]. Such a metric more clearly reflects the accuracy of the forecast than does the mean error because in the RMSE, overestimates and underestimates do not offset one another. The RMSE not only indicates the size of the overall discrepancy without regard to its direction, but it also gives greater weight to larger errors than does the mean error.

In its analysis, CBO first established a base case against which to assess the effectiveness of alternative forecasting methodologies. Using the simplified model, CBO identified the RMSEs for each liabilities projection year, making no adjustment to account for the error in the alignment year. The RMSE in the alignment year in that base case was 2.1 percent of the estimate of liabilities from the model; the RMSE was 4.1 percent in the first projection year (see Table B-1 on page 26). The error grew steadily over the first few years before leveling off at 14.7 percent of liabilities in the final (seventh) projection year.

CBO then measured RMSEs under three general approaches: carrying forward the alignment-year error into the estimates for subsequent years, using multiple years of tax return data from the IRS (rather than only the most recent year of available Statistics of Income data), and combining those two methods. Approaches that reduced RMSEs would be judged as increasing the accuracy of CBO's projections.

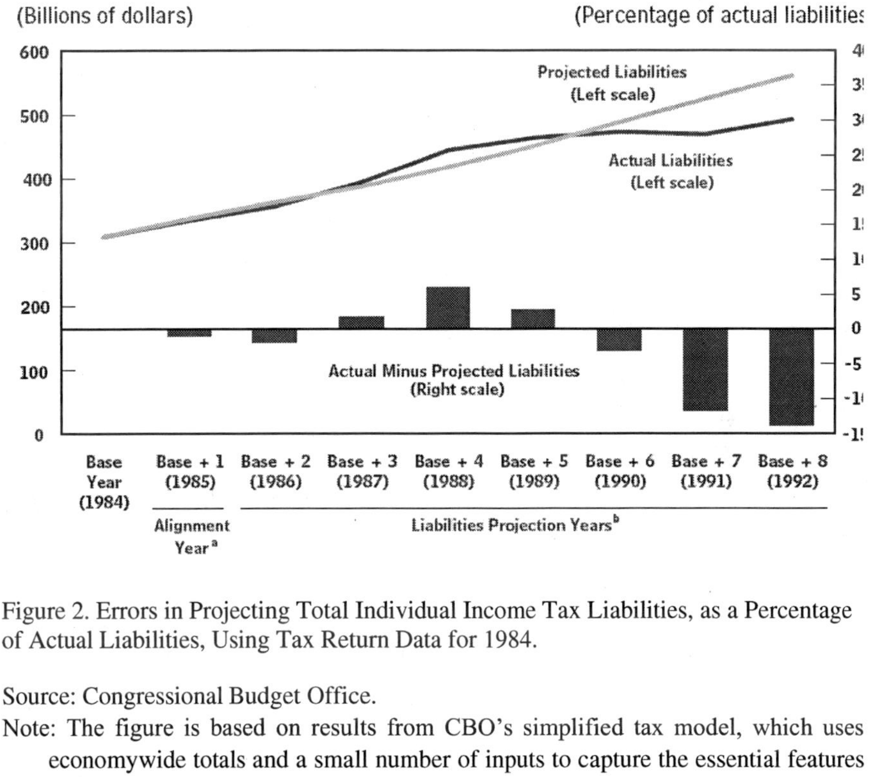

Figure 2. Errors in Projecting Total Individual Income Tax Liabilities, as a Percentage of Actual Liabilities, Using Tax Return Data for 1984.

Source: Congressional Budget Office.

Note: The figure is based on results from CBO's simplified tax model, which uses economywide totals and a small number of inputs to capture the essential features of CBO's more detailed microsimulation method.

[a] The alignment year is a year for which total tax receipts are known but detailed tax statistics are not yet available. The actual results for that year can be used to create an adjustment for the rest of the projection horizon by comparing the results from CBO's model for that year with actual individual income tax liabilities and then adjusting the model's projections for the remaining years of the forecast by that first-year difference.

[b] Projection years in the model representing the years in which tax liabilities are incurred, regardless of when payment is made.

Table 1. Errors in Projecting Liabilities, as a Percentage of Actual Liabilities

Base Year [a]	Liability Year for Which the Projection Was Made[b]							
	Base Year + 1	Base Year + 2	Base Year + 3	Base Year + 4	Base Year + 5	Base Year + 6	Base Year + 7	Base Year + 8
1984	-1.0	-1.9	1.7	6.1	2.8	-3.2	-11.7	-13.9
1985	-1.8	0.6	6.1	3.8	-1.5	-9.0	-10.3	-14.3
1986	1.3	5.1	1.1	-3.9	-11.4	-13.1	-18.0	-18.7
1987	4.3	-2.5	-7.0	-15.1	-16.8	-21.6	-22.3	-19.6
1988	-2.4	-4.8	-9.8	-12.1	-18.0	-19.4	-17.2	-12.3
1989	-2.4	-3.4	-2.2	-7.9	-8.8	-6.4	-1.9	3.3
1990	-0.1	3.0	*	-0.6	1.7	6.8	12.9	18.8
1991	-0.3	-2.9	-4.0	-1.8	3.3	9.1	14.5	19.6
1992	-1.9	-3.7	-2.0	4.0	9.9	15.1	20.0	25.0
1993	1.1	1.4	6.8	12.9	18.2	23.0	27.9	17.3
1994	0.7	2.9	7.5	13.2	18.6	24.0	13.0	4.0
1995	0.8	2.0	8.2	14.4	20.8	10.2	1.9	-0.6
1996	1.8	4.2	10.1	16.8	7.0	-0.7	-2.5	5.8
1997	1.4	1.3	7.5	-3.9	-12.7	-14.4	-4.8	3.2
1998	1.3	2.2	-10.4	-21.1	-24.1	-14.1	-5.7	
1999	0.7	-8.9	-15.8	-20.4	-11.6	-3.6		
2000	-3.1	-6.0	-9.3	-2.7	2.9			
2001	-2.5	-2.8	4.0	8.8				
2002	-1.6	4.2	8.8					
2003	3.6	7.6						
2004	3.5							

Source: Congressional Budget Office.

Notes: The table is based on results from CBO's simplified tax model, which uses economywide totals and a small number of inputs to capture the essential features of CBO's more detailed microsimulation method.

Errors are actual liabilities minus projected liabilities, adjusted to remove the effects of legislation enacted after the base year and represented as a percentage of actual liabilities.

Missing values in the table represent years for which actual liabilities are not yet available or for which actual liabilities have not been calculated because of difficulties in making adjustments for enacted legislation.

* = between -0.05 percent and 0.05 percent.

[a] Data on actual liabilities were taken from the samples of tax returns in the Internal Revenue Service's Statistics of Income Individual Income Tax Files published for these years.

[b] The liability year is the calendar year in which the tax liability is incurred, regardless of when payment is made.

Approach 1: Adjusting the Simplified Tax Model's Results for the Alignment-Year Error

Despite the lack of detailed tax return data available beyond the base year, CBO has a good estimate of actual total income tax liabilities for the alignment year based on data from overall tax collections for that year. One way to use that information to improve projections of individual income tax receipts would be to adjust the model's projections for later years by the percentage error in the model's results for the alignment year. For example, the revenue projections that CBO produced in early 1987 were based on the IRS's Statistics of Income file for 1984. CBO recreated that revenue forecast for this analysis, using the STM and the macroeconomic forecast CBO produced in 1987, and found that actual tax liabilities in 1985 were 1 percent less than the projection from the STM.

In January 1987, when CBO was constructing its revenue forecast, analysts would have known that the model had overestimated liabilities by 1 percent in 1985 (the alignment year), but they would not have had detailed data on the actual liabilities for 1985 nor any data on actual liabilities for 1986. With those data now available, it can be seen that the STM was also overestimating liabilities for the first projection year (1986); the error for that year was 1.9 percent. CBO could have reduced that error by adjusting the model's result for 1986 by the amount of the 1985 error, which would have led to an error for 1986 of just less than 1 percent and improved the accuracy of the forecast in that instance.

One simple method for evaluating the effectiveness of adjusting future-year forecasts by the alignment-year error is to consider the number of years in which doing so would improve the forecasting of liabilities. Among the 20 forecasts that CBO considered, making the alignment-year adjustment for each of the seven years in a forecast's projection window reduced the error in forecasting tax liabilities for the first projection year in 15 of those 20 forecasts. That is, it reduced the error in forecasting liabilities for the calendar year immediately preceding the January in which the forecast was being prepared—in the previous example, 1986. Carrying that same adjustment into the second projection year (1987 in the previous example) reduced the forecasting error for that year in 11 of 19 forecasts. However, carrying forward the alignment-year adjustment into years beyond the second year in the liabilities projection window reduced the error in fewer than half of those cases.

For all of the forecasts examined in this analysis, CBO used changes in the RMSE to measure the effect of making the full alignment-year adjustment to estimates for all years in the projection window. CBO found that:

- Using the full alignment-year adjustment for the first year of the projection window *reduced* the RMSE in that year by 12.7 percent (0.5 percentage points; see Figure 3 and Table B-1 on page 26);
- Using the entire alignment-year adjustment for the second year of the projection window *increased* the RMSE by 1.6 percent (0.1 percentage point); and
- Using the alignment-year adjustment for subsequent years in the projection window *increased* the RMSE in those years by about 3 percent (0.4 percentage points).

In sum, adjusting the model's results by the percentage error in the alignment year would have improved CBO's forecast of tax liabilities only for the first year of the projection period. A variant of that approach would be to adjust the model's results by a percentage that was smaller or larger than the alignment-year error. CBO's analysis of such adjustments revealed the following:

- Adjusting future-year results by only 50 percent of the alignment-year error *reduced* the RMSE in the first year of the projection window by 9.4 percent (0.4 percentage points), had no impact in the second year, and *increased* the RMSE by about 1 percent (0.2 percentage points) in subsequent years.
- Adjusting future-year results by 150 percent of the alignment-year error had an effect in the first year similar to that of adjusting the results by 50 percent of the error: The RMSE for the first projection year was *reduced* by 9.3 percent (0.4 percentage points). Using that approach for years beyond the first year of the projection window *increased* errors in those years by amounts ranging from 4.5 percent (0.6 percentage points) to 6.0 percent (0.7 percentage points).

Thus, CBO's analysis indicates that the best way to improve the accuracy of CBO's projections by adjusting the model's results for the alignment-year error is to use an adjustment equal to that error—but only for liabilities in the first year of the projection period.

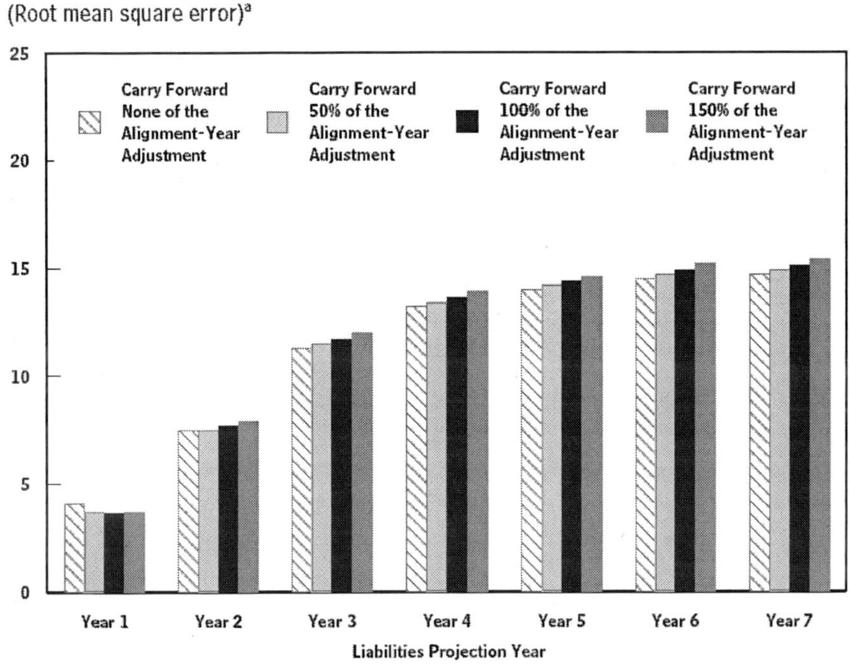

Source: Congressional Budget Office.

Notes: The figure is based on results from CBO's simplified tax model using one (base) year of tax return data. The simplified model uses economywide totals and a small number of inputs to capture the essential features of CBO's more detailed microsimulation method.

The first year after the base year is referred to as the alignment year; for that year, total tax receipts are known but detailed tax statistics are not yet available. The actual results for that year can be used to create an adjustment for the rest of the projection horizon by comparing the results from CBO's model for that year with actual individual income tax liabilities and then adjusting the model's projections for the remaining years of the forecast by that first-year difference.

[a] The root mean square error is calculated by first squaring each of the errors in CBO's projections for a particular forecast year (for example, for the base year + 2, or the first liabilities projection year, as described in the text) and then taking the square root of the arithmetic average of the squared errors. In general, the smaller the error, the more accurate the projection will be.

Figure 3. Effects of Carrying the Alignment-Year Adjustment into All Liabilities Projection Years.

Intuitively, it is reasonable to expect that carrying forward the alignment-year adjustment into the first year of the projection window would generally, although not always, improve the accuracy of CBO's revenue forecast. In a number of forecast periods, many of the sources of error in CBO's revenue projections (such as changes in the distribution of income or in the relationship between income as measured in the NIPAs and income as reported on tax returns) would persist for at least another year.

According to CBO's analysis, however, continuing the alignment-year adjustment (or some portion of it) beyond the first projection year does not generally improve the forecast's accuracy. One reason may be that CBO's projections, like those of most other forecasters, have been most accurate in periods in which the economy and tax liabilities were growing at a steady pace and least accurate when the projections were made at a turning point in the business cycle—that is, at the beginning or end of a recession or economic expansion. Thus, carrying forward the alignment-year adjustment at the beginning of a recession might worsen the forecast's accuracy, not because the source of the initial error was purely random but because the error was the result of an unexpected drop in income as the economy entered a downturn.

Approach 2: Basing Projections on Tax Return Data for Multiple Years

Errors in CBO's individual income tax projections could arise from temporary fluctuations in factors—such as the difference between wages and salaries reported on tax returns and wages and salaries reported in the NIPAs—that can vary from year to year. Using tax return data from years before the base year in addition to the base-year data might smooth those variations and improve the forecast's accuracy. For example, instead of projecting income tax receipts for 2010 solely on the basis of the tax returns filed in 2007, CBO could produce separate estimates—using the same macroeconomic forecast and tax return data from 2006 and 2007 (or even more years)—and then average the results.

CBO therefore analyzed the impact of using multiple years of tax return data, weighted equally, instead of relying solely on data from the most recent year. It found that using tax return data from multiple previous years minimized the impact of minor annual fluctuations in those data and thereby improved the accuracy of its projections. Using four years of tax return data yielded the best overall improvement, reducing the forecasting error in all seven years of the projection period. That approach reduced the RMSE in the first projection year by 9.3 percent (0.4 percentage points) and the RMSE in the second year by 4.9 percent (0.4 percentage points; see Figure 4 and Table B-2 on page 28).[14] The reduction in the RMSE continued to diminish in subsequent years, dropping to 0.3 percent (less than 0.1 percentage point) by the seventh year in the projection window.

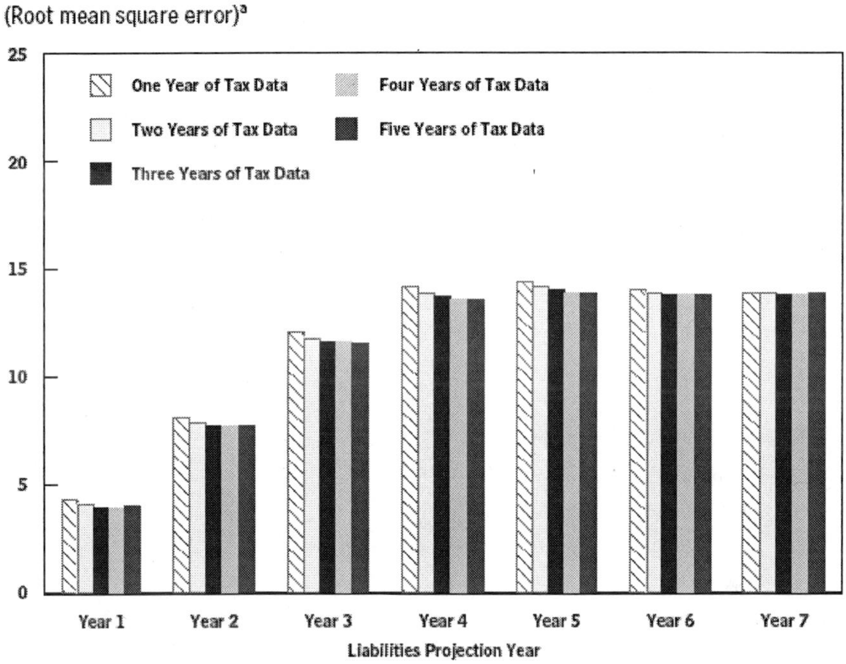

Source: Congressional Budget Office.

Notes: The figure is based on results from CBO's simplified tax model, which uses economywide totals and a small number of inputs to capture the essential features of CBO's more detailed microsimulation method.

The tax return data come from the Internal Revenue Service's yearly Statistics of Income Individual Income Tax Files, which provide detailed information from a sample of tax returns.

a. The root mean square error is calculated by first squaring each of the errors in CBO's projections for a particular forecast year (for example, for the base year + 2, or the first liabilities projection year, as described in the text) and then taking the square root of the arithmetic average of the squared errors. In general, the smaller the error, the more accurate the projection will be.

Figure 4. Effects of Using Multiple Years of Tax Return Data.

CBO found less improvement when it averaged multiple projections that were based on more or fewer than four years of data:

- Moving from a single year of base data to an average of two years of data reduced the RMSE in all projection years except the seventh.
- Compared with using projections based on two years of data, using the average of projections based on three years of data further reduced the RMSE in all projection years—but the reduction from using four years of data was greater.
- Using five years of data did not yield a noticeable reduction in the RMSE in the first projection year compared with the reduction from averaging data over four years, and it marginally increased the error in a number of the later projection years (see Figure 4 and Table B-2 on page 28).

Approach 3: Combining the Methods to Maximize Accuracy

Carrying forward the adjustment for the alignment year or averaging projections based on using several years of tax return information for the base year would each reduce the forecasting error in one or more years of the liabilities projection window. The final approach that CBO examined in this analysis was a combination of the two adjustments, to determine whether that strategy would yield a larger reduction in the forecasting error than the reduction achieved by either method alone. To test that approach, CBO analyzed several different combinations of adjusting for the error in the alignment year and using the average of multiple projections produced from different base years.

Of the options that CBO examined, the combination that was most effective in reducing the RMSE in the estimates of liabilities produced by the STM was to average projections based on the four most recent years of tax return data, carry about 50 percent of the alignment-year adjustment into the first year of the projection window, and make no change to the estimates for subsequent years.[15] That method reduced the RMSE for the first year of the projection window by 17.7 percent (0.7 percentage points; see Figure 5 and Table B-3 on page 30). The method reduced the RMSE for the second year by 5.5 percent (0.4 percentage points) and continued to reduce the error through the seventh year—by 2.1 percent for that year (0.3 percentage points).

Carrying forward 100 percent or 150 percent of the alignment-year adjustment, in combination with averaging projections based on the four most recent years of tax data, reduced the RMSE in estimates of liabilities for the first year of the projection window but by less than did carrying forward only half of the adjustment. In addition, carrying forward all or more than all of the adjustment did not reduce the RMSE uniformly after the first projection year: In combination with averaging projections based on four years of tax data, carrying forward 150 percent of the alignment-year adjustment *increased* the RMSE for all years beyond the first projection year, and carrying forward 100 percent of the adjustment *increased* the RMSE for the final two years of the projection window.

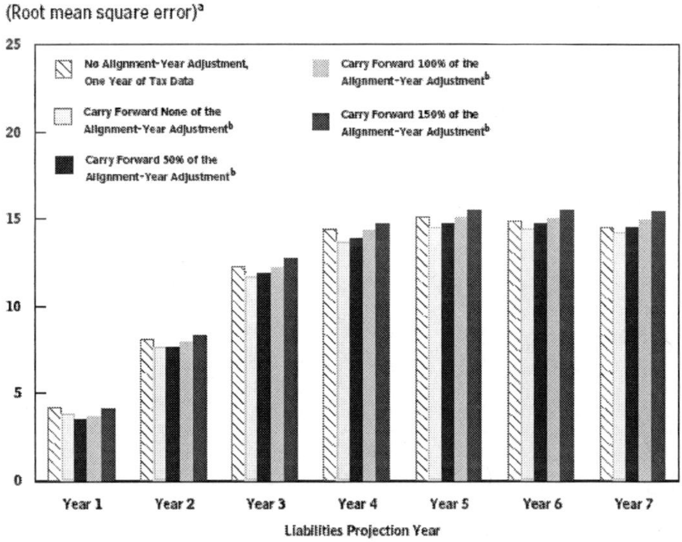

Source: Congressional Budget Office.

Notes: The figure is based on results from CBO's simplified tax model, which uses economywide totals and a small number of inputs to capture the essential features of CBO's more detailed microsimulation method.

The tax return data come from the Internal Revenue Service's yearly Statistics of Income Individual Income Tax Files, which provide detailed information from a sample of individual income tax returns.

The first year after the base year is referred to as the alignment year; for that year, total tax receipts are known but detailed tax statistics are not yet available. The actual results for that year can be used to create an adjustment for the rest of the projection horizon by comparing the results from CBO's model for that year with actual individual income tax liabilities and then adjusting the model's projections for the remaining years of the forecast by that first-year difference.

[a] The root mean square error is calculated by first squaring each of the errors in CBO's projections for a particular forecast year (for example, for the base year + 2, or the first liabilities projection year, as described in the text) and then taking the square

root of the arithmetic average of the squared errors. In general, the smaller the error, the more accurate the projection will be.

[b] In these cases, CBO used the four most recent years of tax return data available.

Figure 5. Effects of Carrying the Alignment-Year Adjustment into All Liabilities Projection Years and Using Four Years of Tax Return Data.

The findings presented here have limitations, however, in large part because they are based on results from the STM over a relatively small number of years. As a result, they may reflect the events that occurred during that period but not be representative of the range of outcomes likely to occur in the future. For example, the particularly severe recession of 2007 to 2009 was outside the period covered by the analysis, and the errors in CBO's revenue projections during the recession were much larger than those during the period that this analysis included. Nevertheless, the analysis period included several events—such as the 1990–1991 and 2001 recessions and the economic boom of the late 1990s—that might well be representative of the kinds of ups and downs most likely to lead to large forecasting errors in the future.

APPENDIX A: CBO'S SIMPLIFIED TAX MODEL

The simplified tax model (STM) that the Congressional Budget Office (CBO) developed for this analysis uses economywide totals and a small number of inputs to reflect the essential features of the microsimulation method that CBO uses for its official revenue forecasts.

Key Features

The STM comprises two modules, one for projecting liabilities from realizations of capital gains and another for projecting liabilities from all other sources of income. In the STM, estimates of tax liabilities other than from capital gains realizations are a function of several key inputs (see Table A-1); those inputs include the following:

- *Income.* Tax liabilities in the STM vary with the key components of income— wages, interest, dividends, and proprietors' income (capital gains are handled separately). CBO derived the totals for those components for the base year from the tax return data for that year; it derived those totals for subsequent years by increasing the base-year amounts by the estimated rate of growth of taxable personal income.[1]

- *Average Tax Rate for the Base Year*. The average tax rate is the ratio of taxes paid to income for all taxpayers in the base year. As with income, the calculation of the average tax rate excludes capital gains realizations and the taxes collected on those gains.
- *Tax Elasticities with Respect to Real Income Growth and Inflation.* In the STM, projected changes in the average tax rate from the rate in the base year are calculated on the basis of estimated changes in real (inflation-adjusted) income growth and inflation. The major parameters of the income tax—such as the brackets, the personal exemptions, and the standard deduction—are indexed for inflation to prevent average tax rates from rising when income grows solely as a result of a general rise in prices. However, if income grows faster than the rate of inflation, more income will be taxed at higher rates, which will cause the average tax rate to rise over time. Similarly, if income grows more slowly than the rate of inflation, less income will be taxed at higher rates, which will cause the average tax rate to fall over time. In addition, not all parameters of the tax system are indexed for inflation; therefore, a general uptick in prices can also cause average tax rates to rise.[2]

  The relationship between the percentage change in the average tax rate and the percentage change in other variables, such as real income per capita and the level of prices, is summarized in terms of elasticities—that is, the ratio of those changes. CBO simulated the impact of increases in real and nominal income for each base year using the tax return data that underlie its more detailed microsimulation model to determine how increases in real income and the price level affect tax liabilities. It then used those year-specific elasticities, which change over time as a result of alterations in the tax code and in the income distribution, as inputs for the STM.

All of the above inputs are combined to produce a forecast of tax liabilities other than those from capital gains realizations. The latter are excluded because liabilities resulting from capital gains realizations are determined by a different schedule of tax rates than that for most other forms of income. Consequently, in this analysis, CBO used a separate module to forecast such liabilities under the assumption that the amount of capital gains is known for the two years following the base year.

Table A-1. Key Inputs for CBO's Simplified Tax Model

Base Year[a]	Adjusted Gross Income[b] (Billions of dollars)	Average Tax Rate[c] (Percent)	Tax Elasticity with Respect to[d]	
			Real Growth per Capita[e]	Inflation
1984	2,081	13.5	1.71	1.05
1985	2,234	13.4	1.72	1.06
1986	2,345	13.4	1.70	1.04
1987	2,625	12.8	1.67	1.09
1988	2,920	12.8	1.56	1.07
1989	3,102	12.8	1.56	1.03
1990	3,283	12.8	1.55	1.00
1991	3,353	12.6	1.57	1.00
1992	3,502	12.8	1.55	1.05
1993	3,571	13.1	1.57	1.03
1994	3,755	13.3	1.56	1.03
1995	4,009	13.6	1.56	1.04
1996	4,275	13.8	1.54	1.01
1997	4,605	14.2	1.53	1.05
1998	4,961	14.1	1.54	1.06
1999	5,303	14.4	1.52	1.07
2000	5,721	14.9	1.50	1.08
2001	5,821	13.5	1.57	1.11
2002	5,765	13.0	1.61	1.17
2003	5,884	11.6	1.63	1.22
2004	6,292	12.1	1.59	1.22
2005	6,737	12.4	1.56	1.23

Source: Congressional Budget Office.

Note: CBO's simplified tax model uses economywide totals and a small number of inputs to capture the essential features of CBO's more detailed microsimulation method.

[a] The table is based on detailed data from the samples of tax returns in the Internal Revenue Service's Statistics of Income Individual Income Tax Files published for these years.

[b] Adjusted gross income—in this case, excluding capital gains—is calculated by subtracting deductions and other adjustments from a person's gross income.

[c] Calculated as taxes on income divided by income, both excluding capital gains and losses.

[d] An elasticity is a measure of the relationship between two variables—specifically, the ratio of the percentage change in one variable to the percentage change in the other.

[e] Growth in inflation-adjusted income per person.

For the first few years of each forecast horizon during the 1984–2005 period, CBO estimated capital gains realizations through a regression analysis based primarily on changes in the amount of businesses' fixed investment (for example, in structures and software) and the recent performance of the stock market relative to potential GDP, as well as changes in the rate at which gains are taxed.[3] For the latter years of a forecast horizon, CBO projected that capital gains realizations (and hence the resulting tax liabilities) would revert to a level consistent with their long-term relationship to GDP, which varies with the tax rates in effect.

COMPARISON WITH CBO'S MICROSIMULATION MODEL

In addition to its use of aggregated data, the STM differs in other respects from the microsimulation model used in CBO's official forecasting process. For example, the usual forecasting method uses detailed projections of the population, disaggregated by age, sex, and marital status, to account for the growth of various demographic groups represented in the base year of tax return data. In contrast, the STM implicitly incorporates the assumption that the population growth rate is the same for all such groups (and thus all returns). Although the resulting projections from the STM will differ from the estimates produced using the microsimulation model, the difference introduced by the simplifying assumption of one growth rate is small, especially over the forecast horizons that CBO analyzes here.

Another difference between the two models is the way they treat the growth of certain types of taxable income, such as pension income and distributions from individual retirement accounts. The full microsimulation model projects the growth of each type of income separately, whereas the STM simply uses the rate of growth of overall taxable personal income (which includes such components as wages, interest, and dividends), excluding capital gains. The methodology used to project capital gains closely approximates the methodology that CBO ordinarily uses for such estimates.

Unlike projections from CBO's microsimulation model, the projections from the STM do not reflect changes in the tax code. As a result, CBO adjusted the STM's results for the effects of legislation enacted between the base year and a projection year before comparing those estimates with actual tax liabilities.[4]

Like the projections generated by CBO's microsimulation model, those from the STM were based on the macroeconomic forecast that CBO produced when it made its revenue projections. For example, in evaluating the projections that were based on actual tax return data for liabilities in 1984, CBO used its macroeconomic estimates from January 1987. The STM projections do not incorporate currently available data for the macroeconomic variables. As a result, CBO's analysis takes into account the errors that result from inaccuracies in the underlying macroeconomic forecast.

Despite several differences between the two approaches, the STM produces errors similar to those produced using the microsimulation model, thus permitting analysts to assess the effects of using different methods for incorporating available information from the recent past.[5] The STM also provides a tool for analyzing the impact of some of the assumptions CBO uses in forecasting. By comparison with the microsimulation model, however, the STM can more easily be used for each base year without additional adjustments.

APPENDIX B: DETAILED DATA FROM THE ANALYSIS

This appendix comprises Tables B-1, B-2, and B-3, which provide the underlying data for Figures 3, 4, and 5 in the main text.

Table B-1. Effects on Root Mean Square Errors in CBO's Simplified Tax Model from Carrying Forward the Alignment-Year Adjustment

Liabilities Projection Horizon	Number of Revenue Forecasts Providing Data[a]	RMSE with No Alignment-Year Adjustment[b]	With Alignment-Year Adjustment[b]		
			RMSE	Percentage-Point Change	Percentage Change
			Carry Forward 50 Percent of the Adjustment		
Alignment Year	21	2.1	2.1	n.a.	n.a.
Projection Year 1	20	4.1	3.7	-0.4	-9.4
Projection Year 2	19	7.5	7.5	*	*
Projection Year 3	18	11.3	11.5	0.2	1.3
Projection Year 4	17	13.2	13.4	0.2	1.2
Projection Year 5	16	14.0	14.2	0.2	1.1
Projection Year 6	15	14.5	14.7	0.2	1.3
Projection Year 7	14	14.7	14.9	0.2	1.2
			Carry Forward 100 Percent of the Adjustment		
Alignment Year	21	2.1	2.1	n.a.	n.a.
Projection Year 1	20	4.1	3.6	-0.5	-12.7
Projection Year 2	19	7.5	7.7	0.1	1.6
Projection Year 3	18	11.3	11.7	0.4	3.4
Projection Year 4	17	13.2	13.6	0.4	2.9
Projection Year 5	16	14.0	14.4	0.4	2.7
Projection Year 6	15	14.5	14.9	0.4	2.9
Projection Year 7	14	14.7	15.1	0.4	2.9

Table B-1. (Continued)

Liabilities Projection Horizon	Number of Revenue Forecasts Providing Data[a]	RMSE with No Alignment-Year Adjustment[b]	With Alignment-Year Adjustment[b]		
			RMSE	Percentage-Point Change	Percentage Change
Alignment Year	21	2.1	2.1	n.a.	n.a.
Projection Year 1	20	4.1	3.7	-0.4	-9.3
Projection Year 2	19	7.5	7.9	0.4	4.8
Projection Year 3	18	11.3	12.0	0.7	6.0
Projection Year 4	17	13.2	13.9	0.7	5.0
Projection Year 5	16	14.0	14.6	0.6	4.5
Projection Year 6	15	14.5	15.2	0.7	4.9
Projection Year 7	14	14.7	15.4	0.7	4.8

Source: Congressional Budget Office.

Notes: CBO's simplified tax model uses economywide totals and a small number of inputs to capture the essential features of CBO's more detailed microsimulation method.

The first year after the base year of actual data from the Internal Revenue Service is referred to as the alignment year. For that year, total tax receipts are known, but detailed tax statistics are not yet available. The actual results for that year can be used to create an adjustment for the rest of the projection horizon by comparing the results from CBO's model for that year with actual individual income tax liabilities and then adjusting the model's projections for the remaining years of the forecast by that first-year difference.

The root mean square error is calculated by first squaring each of the errors in CBO's projections for a particular forecast year (for example, for the base year + 2, or the first liabilities projection year, as described in the text) and then taking the square root of the arithmetic average of the squared errors. In general, the smaller the error, the more accurate the projection will be.

RSME = root mean square error; n.a. = not applicable; * = between -0.05 percent and 0.05 percent.

[a] CBO's 10-year revenue forecasts for 1984 through 2005.

[b] Results are based on one year of actual tax return data.

Table B-2. Effects on Root Mean Square Errors in CBO's Simplified Tax Model from Using Multiple Years of Tax Return Data

Liabilities Projection Horizon	Number of Revenue Forecasts Providing Data[a]	RMSE with One Year of Tax Return Data	With Multiple Years of Tax Return Data		
			RMSE	Percentage-Point Change	Percentage Change
			Use Two Years of Tax Data		
Projection Year 1	16	4.3	4.1	-0.2	-5.1
Projection Year 2	15	8.1	7.9	-0.2	-2.5
Projection Year 3	14	12.1	11.8	-0.3	-2.5
Projection Year 4	13	14.2	13.9	-0.3	-2.1
Projection Year 5	12	14.4	14.2	-0.2	-1.5
Projection Year 6	11	14.0	13.9	-0.1	-0.8
Projection Year 7	10	13.9	13.9	*	*
			Use Three Years of Tax Data		
Projection Year 1	16	4.3	3.9	-0.4	-8.7
Projection Year 2	15	8.1	7.7	-0.4	-4.6
Projection Year 3	14	12.1	11.6	-0.5	-4.1
Projection Year 4	13	14.2	13.7	-0.5	-3.5
Projection Year 5	12	14.4	14.0	-0.4	-2.7
Projection Year 6	11	14.0	13.8	-0.2	-1.4
Projection Year 7	10	13.9	13.8	*	-0.3
			Use Four Years of Tax Data		
Projection Year 1	16	4.3	3.9	-0.4	-9.3
Projection Year 2	15	8.1	7.7	-0.4	-4.9

Table B-2. (Continued)

Liabilities Projection Horizon	Number of Revenue Forecasts Providing Data[a]	RMSE with One Year of Tax Return Data	With Multiple Years of Tax Return Data		
			RMSE	Percentage-Point Change	Percentage Change
Projection Year 3	14	12.1	11.6	-0.6	-4.8
Projection Year 4	13	14.2	13.6	-0.6	-4.2
Projection Year 5	12	14.4	13.9	-0.4	-3.0
Projection Year 6	11	14.0	13.8	-0.2	-1.5
Projection Year 7	10	13.9	13.8	*	-0.3
Projection Year 1	16	4.3	4.0	-0.4	-8.2
Projection Year 2	15	8.1	7.7	-0.4	-4.7
Projection Year 3	14	12.1	11.5	-0.6	-5.2
Projection Year 4	13	14.2	13.6	-0.6	-4.5
Projection Year 5	12	14.4	13.9	-0.5	-3.3
Projection Year 6	11	14.0	13.8	-0.2	-1.7
Projection Year 7	10	13.9	13.9	*	-0.1

Source: Congressional Budget Office.

Notes: CBO's simplified tax model uses economywide totals and a small number of inputs to capture the essential features of CBO's more detailed microsimulation method.

The root mean square error is calculated by first squaring each of the errors in CBO's projections for a particular forecast year (for example, for the base year + 2, or the first liabilities projection year, as described in the text) and then taking the square root of the arithmetic average of the squared errors. In general, the smaller the error, the more accurate the projection will be.

RSME = root mean square error; * = between -0.05 percent and 0.05 percent.

[a] CBO's 10-year revenue forecasts for 1984 through 2005.

Table B-3. Effects on Root Mean Square Errors in CBO's Simplified Tax Model from Carrying the Alignment-Year Adjustment into All Liabilities Projection Years and Using Four Years of Tax Return Data

Liabilities Projection Horizon	Number of Revenue Forecasts Providing Data[a]	RMSE with No Alignment-Year Adjustment[b]	With Alignment-Year Adjustment[c]		
			RMSE	Percentage- Point Change	Percentage Change
			Carry Forward None of the Adjustment		
Alignment Year	18	2.6	2.6	n.a.	n.a.
Projection Year 1	17	4.2	3.8	-0.4	-9.8
Projection Year 2	16	8.1	7.6	-0.4	-5.5
Projection Year 3	15	12.3	11.7	-0.7	-5.4
Projection Year 4	14	14.4	13.7	-0.7	-4.9
Projection Year 5	13	15.1	14.5	-0.6	-4.2
Projection Year 6	12	14.9	14.4	-0.4	-3.0
Projection Year 7	11	14.5	14.2	-0.3	-2.1
			Carry Forward 50 Percent of the Adjustment		
Alignment Year	18	2.6	2.6	n.a.	n.a.
Projection Year 1	17	4.2	3.5	-0.7	-17.7
Projection Year 2	16	8.1	7.6	-0.4	-5.4
Projection Year 3	15	12.3	11.9	-0.5	-3.7
Projection Year 4	14	14.4	13.9	-0.5	-3.4
Projection Year 5	13	15.1	14.7	-0.4	-2.7
Projection Year 6	12	14.9	14.7	-0.2	-1.3

Table B-3. (Continued)

Liabilities Projection Horizon	Number of Revenue Forecasts Providing Data[a]	RMSE with No Alignment-Year Adjustment[b]	With Alignment-Year Adjustment[c]		
			RMSE	Percentage- Point Change	Percentage Change
Projection Year 7	11	14.5	14.5	*	-0.2
			Carry Forward 100 Percent of the Adjustment		
Alignment Year	18	2.6	2.6	n.a.	n.a.
Projection Year 1	17	4.2	3.6	-0.6	-14.8
Projection Year 2	16	8.1	7.9	-0.2	-2.5
Projection Year 3	15	12.3	12.2	-0.1	-0.8
Projection Year 4	14	14.4	14.3	-0.2	-1.1
Projection Year 5	13	15.1	15.1	-0.1	-0.3
Projection Year 6	12	14.9	15.0	0.2	1.2
Projection Year 7	11	14.5	14.9	0.3	2.4
Alignment Year	18	2.6	2.6	n.a.	n.a.
Projection Year 1	17	4.2	4.1	-0.1	-2.2
Projection Year 2	16	8.1	8.3	0.2	3.0
Projection Year 3	15	12.3	12.7	0.4	3.2
Projection Year 4	14	14.4	14.7	0.3	2.0
Projection Year 5	13	15.1	15.5	0.4	2.8

Liabilities Projection Horizon	Number of Revenue Forecasts Providing Data[a]	RMSE with No Alignment-Year Adjustment[b]	With Alignment-Year Adjustment[c]		
			RMSE	Percentage- Point Change	Percentage Change
Projection Year 6	12	14.9	15.5	0.7	4.5
Projection Year 7	11	14.5	15.4	0.8	5.7

Source: Congressional Budget Office.

Notes: CBO's simplified tax model uses economywide totals and a small number of inputs to capture the essential features of CBO's more detailed microsimulation method.

The first year after the base year of actual data from the Internal Revenue Service is referred to as the alignment year. For that year, total tax receipts are known, but detailed tax statistics are not yet available. The actual results for that year can be used to create an adjustment for the rest of the projection horizon by comparing the results from CBO's model for that year with actual individual income tax liabilities and then adjusting the model's projections for the remaining years of the forecast by that first-year difference.

The root mean square error is calculated by first squaring each of the errors in CBO's projections for a particular forecast year (for example, for the base year + 2, or the first liabilities projection year, as described in the text) and then taking the square root of the arithmetic average of the squared errors. In general, the smaller the error, the more accurate the projection will be.

Data in the table that appear in boldface type reflect the combination of methods that was most effective in reducing the RMSE in the estimates of liabilities produced by CBO's simplified tax model.

RSME = root mean square error; n.a. = not applicable; * = between -0.05 percent and 0.05 percent.

[a] CBO's 10-year revenue forecasts for 1984 through 2005.

[b] Results are based on one year of actual tax return data.

[c] Results are based on the four most recent years of tax return data available.

End Notes

[1] CBO produces projections of federal revenues but does not estimate the revenue effects of individual pieces of legislation. That latter task is carried out by the staff of the Joint Committee on Taxation. CBO usually updates its baseline projections of revenues and spending in March and August; this analysis focuses on the projections that CBO releases in January.

[2] For example, an overestimate of 5 percent for one year and either an overestimate or underestimate of 3 percent for another year would produce a mean absolute error of 4 percent. If the calculation for the current year had included projections for years before fiscal year 1997, the mean absolute error would be smaller than 0.4 percent of GDP.

[3] Unlike the calculation of mean absolute errors, calculations of net errors incorporate the offsetting effects of positive and negative differences. Thus, a 5 percent overestimate for one year and a 3 percent underestimate for another year would produce an average net error of 1 percent.

[4] CBO's individual income tax model is a stylized representation of the economy that relies on various simplifying assumptions; as such, it cannot capture all of the determinants of the taxes that people owe. CBO's projections of individual income tax revenues thus combine information from the individual income tax model with the most recent available data on tax collections.

[5] See Alan J. Auerbach, "On the Performance and Use of Government Revenue Forecasts," *National Tax Journal*, vol. 52, no. 4 (December 1999), pp. 767–782; and Rudolph G. Penner, "Federal Revenue Forecasting," in Penner, *Handbook of Government Budget Forecasting* (New York: Taylor & Francis, March 2008). See also George A. Plesko, "The Accuracy of Government Forecasts and Budget Projections," *National Tax Journal,* vol. 41, no. 2 (December 1988), pp. 483–501. All three studies considered projections of total revenues rather than projections of individual income tax revenues. The Plesko study found that, after legislative changes were taken into account, CBO's revenue forecasts were equally likely to be too high as too low, but it did not examine the correlation of errors.

[6] The liability year is the calendar year in which the tax liability is incurred, regardless of when payment is made.

[7] CBO supplements the data from tax returns with information from the Census Bureau's Current Population Survey to account for families that do not file tax returns. For a more detailed discussion of CBO's methods for projecting receipts from individual income taxes, see Congressional Budget Office, *Description of CBO's Models and Methods for Projecting Federal Revenues* (May 2001).

[8] The NIPAs, which are maintained by the Department of Commerce's Bureau of Economic Analysis, track the level and composition of historical U.S. gross domestic product, the prices of its components, and the way in which the costs of production are distributed as income.

[9] At this point in the forecasting process, CBO also has available preliminary data from 2009 tax returns for selected components of income, deductions, and tax liabilities, but those data generally do not supply much additional information beyond that available from the tax collections.

[10] CBO's revenue projections also incorporated information from recent tax collections beyond that used to derive liabilities for 2008. For example, the revenue projections that CBO released in 2010 incorporated data about tax collections in 2009, which provided partial information about tax liabilities for that year. However, assessing the value of using that

additional information from recent collections to improve CBO's projections was beyond the scope of this analysis.

[11] Twice a year, in January and in August, CBO publishes a macroeconomic forecast (including projections for such variables as GDP, components of national income, interest rates, and inflation) that it uses to project federal revenues and spending.

[12] The average tax rate is the ratio, for all taxpayers, of taxes paid to income.

[13] An elasticity is a measure of the relationship between two variables—specifically, the ratio of the percentage change in one variable to the percentage change in another.

[14] The results in this section differ slightly from the results in the previous section on the impact of the alignment-year adjustment because the use of multiple years of data means that fewer forecasts can be analyzed. Thus, for example, the RMSE for the first liabilities projection year shown in Figure 3 and Table B-1 is 4.1 percent and was constructed from 20 forecasts. The RMSE for the same projection year shown in Figure 4 and Table B-2 (the case using one year of tax return data) is 4.3 percent and was constructed from 16 forecasts.

[15] A more detailed analysis for the first projection year, which checked each integer between 50 percent and 100 percent, showed that carrying forward 62 percent of the alignment-year adjustment led to the smallest RMSE (3.47 percent). However, that error did not differ significantly from the RMSE generated by carrying forward 50 percent of the alignment-year error to the first projection year (3.48 percent).

End Notes for Appendix I

[1] CBO's analysis measured income as the sum of the components of taxable personal income in the national income and product accounts—wages and salaries, proprietors' income, interest, and dividends—which were weighted to reflect their shares of taxable income as reported on tax returns.

[2] For example, the thresholds for taxing Social Security benefits are not indexed for inflation. When income rises with inflation, a greater share of benefits is subject to tax, and the tax rate on total income (including benefits) rises as well. The parameters of the alternative minimum tax also are not indexed for inflation, which results in a similar effect.

[3] Potential GDP refers to the level of GDP that corresponds to a high level of resource (labor and capital) use and that neither adds to nor subtracts from inflationary pressures. It is never observed directly and must thus be estimated.

[4] A significant amount of uncertainty surrounds the effects of tax legislation on tax liabilities. In its analysis, CBO relied on published projections of the effects of changes in the tax code at the time the various laws were enacted and did not adjust those estimates to reflect subsequent information about a law's actual effects. (The estimates also reflected the impact of legislation that was enacted before the base year but that had provisions whose effects were phased in over time.) However, those published estimates were on a fiscal year basis, and in some cases, the periods covered by the estimates did not correspond to CBO's forecasting periods. As a result, CBO shifted the estimates to a liability year basis and, when necessary, extended them by producing estimates for additional years.

[5] CBO compared the results of the STM with its projections of revenues from the microsimulation model, which exclude the effects of legislative changes occurring after the base year of data. Over each forecast horizon that CBO examined, the correlation between the forecasting errors for projections of liabilities produced by the STM and the forecasting

errors for projections produced using the microsimulation methodology was roughly 0.9, suggesting that the STM successfully replicated the results of that more complex methodology.

INDEX

H

I

J

L

M

T

U

V

W

Y